A Painter's Pilgrimage

A Painter's Pilgrimage

by Raphael Soyer

*an account of a journey
with drawings by the author*

Crown Publishers, Inc.   New York

For Jean and Tim
in friendship
Raphael Soyer
1984. N.Y.

© 1962 by Raphael Soyer

Library of Congress Catalog Card Number: 62-13782

Printed in the United States of America

Acknowledgments

Grateful acknowledgment for permission to reproduce drawings is hereby given to the Bernhardt Crystal Art Galleries, Inc. of New York City; to Mr. Louis Harrow of Mount Vernon, New York; to Mr. William Meyers of Roslyn, New York and to Mr. Joseph J. Schwartz of Mt. Vernon, New York.

Plates:

A Painter's Pilgrimage

Foreword

Last summer I decided to get away from work and the turmoil of New York for an extended vacation in Europe. That time should not weigh too heavily on my hands, I gave myself a project—to keep a journal in words and pictures.

I have always enjoyed the books on art by the artists themselves— *The Letters of Van Gogh,* for instance, Delacroix's *Journal,* Gaugin's *Noa Noa.* I like compilations of artists' statements, opinions, aphorisms on art such as Robert Goldwater's and Marco Treves's *Artists on Art.* My favorite art histories are John Rewald's of Impressionism and Post-Impressionism, because they are filled with such content.

When I returned to New York and put my drawings and daily entries in order, I was somewhat amazed that I had been able to realize my project, especially the text part of it; it was something I had never tried before.

This is not a world-shaking document; it was not meant to be—it is an expression of one artist's views on art. It is more or less spontaneous, for it was not really planned. It is haphazard . . . personal . . . intimate . . . not too . . . I hope . . . that's it.

May 15, 1961

It is a little over an hour now that I am in the jet bound for London. Over the loudspeaker the invisible captain called our attention to icebergs below. I can spot them way down through rents of the clouds. They look like jagged white marbles. Flying in the jet is not as smooth as I was led to believe. Vibration and motor noise are constant. It may be so because I am sitting in the back.

It is 12:30 now. Four more hours to go. For fifty cents I am served a scotch and soda.

A week ago Monday I finished a small painting of a reclining nude, cleaned my palette and brushes and put my studio in order. I closed shop, so to speak. The six days that followed were slow and tedious. Sleep became nightmarish. I was tormented by fears of flying across the Atlantic and of the impending loneliness (Rebecca will not join me for a month) which I knew would not be dispelled by visits to the many European museums.

Well, here I am in the jet anyway, above the clouds, sipping my second scotch and soda; a lot of conversation is going on, but I have not as yet had the opportunity or the inclination to say "boo" to anybody.

Long ago, this morning to be exact, my wife Rebecca, my daughter Mary and my son-in-law Arnie accompanied me to Idlewild in Mary and Arnie's Volkswagen. Mary and Arnie had to leave soon for work. Rebecca, of course, stayed till I entered the jet. I shall meet them all in Paris next month.

One more hour to London. Time does pass. Am beginning to have faith in the jet. It is an honest, powerful, dependable machine. Above is a deep blue sky, below is a thick blanket of lavender clouds, and below the clouds I guess is the Atlantic.

13

May 16

Called up an acquaintance from New York, the art dealer Julius Weitzner, whose daughter once painted in my studio under my supervision, telling him that I am in London. He promptly invited me to dinner Friday, May 19th.

My first full day in London was spent in the National Gallery. The collection will grow upon me from day to day. What is there left to say about Rembrandt any more? One can only sit in long and deep contemplation in front of the three portraits of old men, the one of himself in the center.

Van Eyck's "Giovanni Arnolfini and His Wife" is abstract, stark and opaque. Compared to it, Vermeer is pure genre and Holbein's "Ambassadors" glow with life. It is lusterless, sparkless, devoid of "flesh tones." The high lights are suppressed. The man with his ashen face, the doll-like wife and toy-like dog are inanimate. The gestures frozen. All is still and airless.

May 17

Last night I called the young English painter J. B. Bratby (I saw an exhibition of his work in New York—I was impressed by it—vital, free, non-conforming), and told the woman who answered that I am a New York painter, that I am acquainted with his work, and that I would like to meet him. The woman asked me to hold on, and soon her shyly excited voice was saying, "Mr. Bratby said he is interested in New York, and would like you to come." "When may I come?" I asked. "Any time. Mr. Bratby never goes out, he always works."

This morning when I got into the taxi the driver anxiously told me that Bratby's address is on the outskirts of London, that the fare would amount to a considerable sum, and in the nice helpful British way advised me that I would do better to go by train. When we got to the gate of Bratby's house I made an arrangement with this man to call for me in an hour. A short stocky young woman with wide open blue or gray eyes, red nose, disheveled hair opened the gate. Her legs were stockingless and muddy. She greeted me shyly and I didn't see her again. Two boys were about, one a four-year-old, the other a bare-legged blond toddler. Both were lightly clad, although it was quite raw.

Then Bratby came out, bearded but very young-looking, his even, pale complexion accentuated by red lips, small brown eyes behind thick, horn-rimmed glasses, high forehead with long, soft dark brown hair. The part of his face above his eyes, just forehead and hair, which he is already beginning to lose, made me think of Cézanne's self-portraits. He brought out chairs and we sat down; the sun reappeared from behind the clouds every now and then. Bratby began to ask about New York—the art situation, galleries, etc. He told me that he paints all the time, that he has a problem—that of over-production—an unusual thing in Great Britain where preciousness and sterility in art are traditional.

Although he sells a great deal and at the moment is well off, in fact very well off, especially considering that he is only thirty-two, he would want to create "another market" for his work, a "New York market," since Great Britain cannot absorb all his paintings. The amount of work he can put out is "preposterous." His studios—there are a few on the premises—are filled with as yet unsold paintings and drawings.

For the present he has decided to refrain from painting except for a portrait commission now and then (on the way out he called my attention to such a portrait hanging on a wall—a striking full-length one of a man), and to write novels instead. One novel, *Breakdown,* if I remember the title correctly, has already been published, he said. He has by now written five novels. "They will all be published." When he smiled his white even teeth showed, he looked very young and at moments kind of idiotic. When he listened, or was thoughtful, his face would age, shrink, its expression withdraw, the eyes would close and almost disappear behind the thick glasses, and with his high forehead and beard he would bring to mind a character out of Russian literature.

Eventually we entered one of his studios; it was stacked with paintings, some huge. The "small ones" also were quite large. Something about his work, too, looked Russian to me—some of the faces he painted and the manner of painting brought Burliuk and Grigorief to mind. I mentioned the name of Burliuk to him, saying, "He sometimes paints as thickly as you," but he had never heard of him. I recognized some paintings that had been displayed in New York. He painted them a few years ago. "How do you compose these huge paintings? Do you make preliminary sketches for them?" I asked. "No," he said, "I start with one figure, anywhere on the fresh canvas, then add another and another, etc., without any coherence. At one time I painted everything I saw before me, the model, the objects, the furniture, my own feet on the floor, my painting hand, without composing, in disorder, in fact."

"You're thirty-two now. You'll probably change as you go on," I said, "in your point of view, your state of mind, in technique." "No," he answered emphatically, "I'll always paint like this. I once made an attempt to change but with unsatisfactory results."

He paints very rapidly—the "small" paintings one a day. "My goodness!" I exclaimed. "Think what your output would be in say thirty more years of painting." "Yes, preposterous," he said, and smiled his childish and idiotic smile. In the center of the studio was a big billiard table, occupying most of the space. "This was recently brought in," he said, pointing to it. "I paint in my other studios." The green-covered table with its many balls has already been depicted in many of his recent canvases. He seems to be a Brigitte Bardot fan—for one of the walls in the studio was covered with pictures of her cut from newspapers and magazines.

When the taxi man called for me I expressed a desire to come to see him again. I told him that I would like to sketch him. "Sure," he said, "any time. I always work, I never leave this place. I never go anywhere."

May 18

Am spending most of my time in the National Gallery. Rembrandt's brooding old man in the armchair with his head leaning on his arm is, to me, one of the most satisfying paintings in the world. The deep harmony of browns and reds and still darker browns that border upon black is truly symphonic.

I was never too fond of Rubens. But today something impelled me to open my sketchbook, and draw the beggars of his painting, "St. Bavo," the two big-boned heavy women, each with an infant strapped to her back, each with more babies sucking her breasts and swarming about, stretching her naked fleshy arms for alms. I felt as if a veil fell off my eyes and Rubens' genius revealed itself to me. No gesture, no movement of body, no facial expression was foreign to him. How he expressed the vitality of the flesh, the quivering of muscle, the fierceness with which the clothes accentuate the free and shameless movements of these female bodies, the folds of these stinking rags, kerchiefs, swaddling clothes, the lust for alms, for mother's milk, for life!

In "The Rape of the Sabine Women," lusty, brown men pull, grab, lift the big, pliant, white, bare-bosomed, bare-legged women. There is a wonderful sense of commotion, yelling, squealing, noise—in short a sense of "sound effect" in this painting. No abstracting, tentativeness, "leaving things to the imagination of the onlooker" for Rubens. How he sinned against aesthetics! How tangibly he depicted everything living at its most fecund moment—man, beast, earth. In "Chateau de Steen" the earth itself sprawls and writhes like one of his giant females.

May 19

"It's like the National Gallery," I said as I entered the Weitzner home and saw a Rubens, a Rembrandt, a Madonna by the Master of Flémalle and other paintings on the walls. "Well, not quite," proudly murmured Mr. Weitzner. There were a couple of European art dealers who left before dinner. Chuck Parker, who was a teacher or a curator, or both, at Oberlin College, and I remained. The Weitzners (Mrs. Weitzner is a pianist, a student of Schnabel's) were warmly hospitable. We drank scotch on the rocks and conversed mostly about art and artists. Mr. Parker asked me whether the purpose of my coming to Europe was to hold exhibitions of my work. "No," I answered, "I came here to look at paintings. I am a museum fiend. No," I found a better word: "a museum pilgrim." "A museum pilgrim," repeated Mr. Parker. "I like that!" He seemed interesting and informed.

May 21

Peter De Francia, to whom Bella Fishko wrote about me, asking him to take me around London, and introduce me to some artists, came to my hotel and took me to his studio by bus. It is cold all the time in London—the chilly air seems to irritate the skin, men and women go about with red noses and generally blotchy faces, and the stockingless legs of girls are crimson with cold. It was freezing in Peter's apartment and in his studio above the apartment (he rents a small house and garden).

Peter is a big florid man of forty whose blue eyes are at times questioning, puzzled. He is well informed about politics, art, literature, theater, etc. He is a socially aware man, has friends all over Europe. I repeat he is full of all sorts of information. When the name Kokoschka came up in conversation, De Francia said that he (Kokoschka) is a typically Viennese artist in his color schemes and feelings; as a matter of fact he was greatly influenced by the work of Multspatch, an 18th-century Austrian baroque who painted in lavenders, blues, grays and pinks (Kokoschka's colors). "There is a story," he said, "no doubt apocryphal, that Kokoschka in his youth promptly fainted upon seeing a mural painted by this predecessor of his—so great was his emotional experience." Peter took me upstairs and showed me his own paintings, and slides of a huge painting, commemorating a contemporary uprising or struggle, I think, in Algeria—all good, furious-on-the-surface paintings, but all unresolved, abortive, unfinished. He is completely unsuccessful materially, can't sustain himself on his art at all, and has to lecture and teach for a living. No gallery (he unconvincingly blames his leftism for it) would give him an exhibition. And yet he is as good as, and better than, many artists in London, who do exhibit and live by their art, and whose work is on permanent display in the Tate Gallery. He suggested that I visit Joseph Herman, a good painter according to him. When I mentioned that I visited Bratby, he seemed surprised and displeased and muttered something about Bratby's sensationalism. I didn't tell him I had made another appointment to see Bratby, in fact tomorrow. Peter's remarks did not dissuade me from keeping it, for Bratby interested me very much.

In the evening I met Peter again at a small peace meeting where an American woman spoke about the progressive movement in the United States. She was factual and mildly interesting. Afterwards, Peter, his saucy, charming young girl friend, Susanna Botts, and I went to some pub and had drinks. Peter decided to go to Paris at the end of the week to find a gallery in which to exhibit, since all London gallery doors seemed closed to him. He entrusted me to his girl friend, and instructed her to take me to a woman artist, Frishman, whose dead husband had been a well known and excellent draftsman on the *Simplicissimus*.

My second visit to Bratby. Again his interesting, shy, untidy wife opened the gate and Bratby led me into his studio. Only one little boy was seen around this time—the bigger one; the younger could only be heard, monotonously crying and whining, as if in pain and discomfort, in a nearby room. I asked about the child. "He has the measles," Bratby said. "He already had it when you were here last time, but we didn't know." That chilly day, I remembered, when he was walking about so lightly clad, bare-legged, in fact. "How about him?" I pointed to the older one. "He had it."

Again I was impressed by the amount of Bratby's work, its vigor and vitality, also by its lack of polish, and by its repetitiousness. I thought of his resolve not to change in manner or technique the next thirty years. This thought depressed me. Thirty years more of picture production by even a Van Gogh or a Modigliani above what they had already produced would have been unbearable. . . . He is obsessed by the idea of creating an "American market" for his work. He showed me also his drawings, life-size ones on rolls of paper—all of girls in different postures and dress and different states of dishevellment, but not nude. These huge drawings were crude and searching, some in lead pencil and some in lead pencil and crayon. He talked again about the official encouragement of sterility and preciousness in art in Great Britain. "Isn't it also true of the United States?" he asked. "There is an artist in New York I read about who does one painting a year." "Peter Blume?" I asked. "No," he answered, "his name starts with an H." "Oh, Edward Hopper!" I exclaimed. "Yes, yes," he said, "Edward Hopper. I don't hold it against him that he paints so slowly; as a matter of fact I like his work, judging from reproductions." He also mentioned Grant Wood's "American Gothic" and "Daughters of the Revolution" which he admires, especially the "American Gothic." "I think it is wonderful," he said. "I don't know your work at all. You'll have to excuse me."

Mrs. Bratby shyly and mutely brought in two mugs of coffee. The whining of the sick child continued somewhere nearby. I made two sketches of Bratby, one sitting on a hand-carved wooden claptrap of an armchair with some of his wild figure paintings behind him. He posed without moving, withdrew, became old-looking, didn't talk, and evinced no interest whatsoever in what I was doing.

I liked him for his simplicity, for his not spouting intellectual clichés, for his natural or feigned eccentricity, for his industry. I suspect that he is quite a sophisticate.

In the afternoon I went to the Tate Gallery. Downstairs is a good collection of French Impressionists, Post-Impressionists, single paintings by Munch, Kokoschka, Chagall, and others of the same caliber. The English paintings bored me. I dislike even Turner and Constable. If Turner is a genius, as it is fashionable to claim today, he is the most boring genius that ever was. One good Claude Lorrain for all the Turners. Constable is fussy, literary. One good Corot for all the Constables in the world, his sketches and all. The two early English paintings I liked were by Hogarth: "The Shrimp Girl" and "Hogarth's Servants." Also liked (some more, some less) paintings by Sickert, Augustus John, Gwen John, Nevinson. Of the contemporary artists represented, I remember Bratby, Herman, Passmore (his early, intelligent but too sweet paintings), Lucian Freud (his small intense portrait of Bacon). But the most impressive and best contemporary representational painting there, in my opinion, is "The Meeting" by the Italian Guttuso, vital and strong, with some collage, very functionally applied, of fragments of newspapers and wallpaper. Needless to say there were non-objective paintings galore, a couple of them by Americans, hung on side walls. There was a wilted look about them; they were loosely stretched, the unpainted patches of the canvases were gray and muddy, and the painted parts passive and dull.

In the morning before going to Bratby I sent the following postcard to Paul Robeson, whose address in London was given to me by Peter De Francia:

DEAR PAUL ROBESON,
Many years ago in my brother Moses Soyer's studio, a party took place in your honor. A book on the work of Leonardo da Vinci signed by the artists present was given to you. Do you remember? I was one of the artists. Am now in London and would like to visit you.

RAPHAEL SOYER

Next day I was told that there are rumors that Robeson is in a hospital, or in the Soviet Union. Subsequently the combination of both rumors proved correct. He is in a hospital somewhere in the Soviet Union.

Visited Joseph Herman. Friendly, intelligent, buoyant man. Aware (happily) of the fact that he is one of the accepted artists in London, has a gallery, exhibits and sells. As a matter of fact when I mentioned names of English artists to Bratby, Herman's name among them, Bratby promptly found and gave me a magazine with an article about Herman. That is another trait that I liked in Bratby: he never spoke negatively about his fellow artists. Joseph Herman lived for many years in Wales, isolated, lonely and inspired. His art was formed by that experience. He still paints the Welsh country, the primitive village, the limited life of its inhabitants—squat men and women at work, at meals, in pubs, at rest. Dark and moody paintings. The color too rich and heavy, I thought. "Completely imaginative [the color]," he told me, "not like it really is." I couldn't help feeling that if the color were more factual, the paintings would have been more interesting. I have seen paintings of this sort; they seemed strangely familiar to me—the work of Roualt, Permeke came to mind. As a matter of fact, Peter De Francia described him to me as influenced by Permeke. I think that the Italian Ottone Rosai is of the same type, as is the American painter Kopman. Each, of course, has his own individual flavor. They are real, professional, on a good level, artists. We spoke a great deal about the Russian Constructivists, the Cubists and the Abstract Expressionists. We deplored the predominance of non-objectivism in art at the moment, and tried to find and explain the moral, psychological, the timely reasons for it. We both agreed that contemporary art is in a state of havoc, and that museum directors, art critics, dealers, historians, teachers are to blame for this. I bellyached as usual against the New York museums—the Museum of Modern Art in particular. Herman complained about the art atmosphere in London. One thing he said stuck in my mind, "We in England have many good twenty-year-old artists but very few good forty-year-old artists. Artistically we die at a very early age."

This evening went to see *La Dolce Vita*, the movie that was made so much of in New York. I was disappointed.

Morning spent at the National Gallery. In the afternoon made two drawings at the British Museum of the Elgin Marbles—the same fragments I drew in 1959. Time and weather patinated and abstracted these stony youths and horses. Their being out of place and element—on the walls of a museum rather than on the pediment of the Parthenon— seems to add to their air of detachment and timelessness.

May 27

Went to the National Gallery again. My time in London is getting short. The 31st I shall be in Paris and meet Mary and Arnie. At the museum concentrated again upon my favorite artists, so well represented there: Van Eyck, Rembrandt, Titian, Rubens. They have spoiled my taste for the lesser men—the "little Dutch masters," the Dutch landscape painters, Teniers, Brouwer, Franz Hals, and others. I have no patience for them and have no time. I like the early Velásquez "Christ at the House of Martha." I went to see the wonderful "Water Carrier" by Velásquez at the Apsley House, the two melancholy-tinged Michelangelos, the two Piero della Francescos, the Masaccio, the portraits by Lorenzo Lotto.

In the afternoon met Susanna Bott, who took me to the artist friend of hers, the widow, Mrs. Frishman. She and her architect son live in the usual cold and drafty London apartment, filled with her paintings. I marveled at the vitality of this frail (very ill, I was told) woman. Her expressionistic paintings of Israeli landscapes, of seaports, of still lifes, are vigorous, full of character. In the evening I had dinner with Susanna Bott. We talked mostly about art, the low ebb of it today, in London, in New York, in Paris. Again I put the onus for it upon the Museum of Modern Art in New York. I found myself blaming the New York museum for all that is wrong with contemporary art. My contention was that the devotion of its zealous directors to non-representational art, the promulgation of it with the Museum's modern propaganda facilities and American wealth, have influenced other museum directors, art officials, critics, dealers, collectors, and finally, artists, all over the world. Art today is in an indescribable state of havoc, I said. I expressed the opinion that the only art of our time that will count for something in the future is that which is being done by the few persisting representationalists, not the banal, platitudinous "academicians," but those who make tradition live, go on, and ever renew itself; those who find dynamic, personal, timely ways to depict our civilization and our life. Like the work of Kokoschka, I said, Manzu, Balthus, Guttuso, Siqueiros, Dix, of a few American painters, and the work of course of George Grosz, Orozco, Rivera, Epstein, who so recently died. I was about to blame the Museum for all that is wrong in the world today . . . and suddenly remembered how the sardonic Picasso blamed all misfortunes on the Ecole des Beaux-Arts. There is that haunting description by Alfred Barr, in his biography of Matisse, of a casual meeting on a Paris street corner between Picasso and Matisse on the eve of the Nazi invasion. Matisse, about to flee the invaders, talks unhappily about the state of affairs and Picasso says: "It is the fault of the Ecole des Beaux-Arts." Of course, the Museum of Modern Art is not the Ecole des Beaux-Arts. Or is it? Or becoming it?

"Artistically we die at an early age in England." I can't get Joseph Herman's words out of my mind. I am becoming increasingly aware of artistic frustration in London, limitation of art activity, caste system among the artists, phoniness, loneliness, rejection.

May 28

Ira Moskowitz wrote to Henry Moore that I am in London and would like to meet him. As a result I received a letter from Mrs. Tinsley, secretary to Henry Moore, to call and make an appointment. I hesitated and procrastinated a day before I called. I felt that Mr. Moore will not know me from Adam, that the response was only in deference to Ira, who is compiling, with Sam Shore, a huge volume of drawings in which one of Moore's will be included. But when I told my London friends of my chance to visit Moore and of my reluctance about it, they said, "Go to see him, he is a fine artist, and we hear he is a very nice man." He seems to be respected both as an artist and man. He is not treated lightly in conversation, as other artists are. I called finally last evening. A woman was on the phone. "Is this Mrs. Tinsley?" I asked. "No, Mrs. Tinsley is off week ends." "This is Raphael Soyer, an artist from New York. Mrs. Tinsley wrote to me to call for an appointment."

"Henry dear, it's Mr. Soyer from New York."

Henry Moore's voice on a different phone: "Dear, get me my daybook."

"Henry, tomorrow the man from Holland is coming to look at the drawings."

Mr. Moore's voice: "And in the morning they are coming to look at the small sculptures. Oh, dear!"

And so on, till finally it was arranged for this afternoon. Mr. Moore told me to get the train at the Liverpool Station and to go to Bishop Stortford and then take a taxi.

As I suspected, Mr. Moore, in spite of his consulting his daybook, was not appointment-free when I arrived. (I had hoped I would have time to make a sketch of him—he would have been nice to draw, with his questioning blue eyes, iron-gray hair, ruddy complexion, but it was out of the question.) Two men were there, an important architect, I gathered, probably Dutch, and a man who, I think, was employing him to build a house, and Moore was being commissioned to do a sculpture to decorate the house. Mr. Moore was very friendly, but I felt I was intruding, and was glad that I had told the taxi man to call for me in an hour. When I came, Mr. Moore was about to lead his visitors to his several studios and show them around. I was invited to join the procession. The studios were filled with old and present work. In one big studio there was a huge wood carving he was at the moment engaged upon—a reclining figure typically hole-y. He showed us bones that he collects, talked to us about the beauty of their forms. To some of them he adds particles of clay. There were also some early bronzes, somewhat more naturalistic. I think that he tends progressively toward complete non-objectivism. He would point to a form (sculpture) and ask his two visitors every once in a while, "Is that what you want?" or "Is that what you have in mind?" and would suggest a change here and there or a combination of two forms. At one time the question came up of the danger of a child sticking his head into one of the holes and not being able to extricate it. Well, Mr. Moore said, he could see to it—he could have the holes higher, too high for a child to reach them, or a hole could even be blocked.

The grounds were beautiful. His bronzes—huge male and female figures, sitting or reclining on the lawn, assumed a primordial aspect, became vaguely expressive and moody, for it was toward evening. The house, too, was lovely. A little Cézanne oil of bathers, two Seurat drawings, a Modigliani drawing on the whitewashed walls—everything was costly, but not ostentatious. Moore was offering drinks, when to my great relief the taxi called for me.

Yesterday while at dinner with Susanna Bott, again talking about art and artists, I said, "Susanna, you seem to be a person in your own right. Would it be possible for me to see *your* work?" She invited me for an early lunch today, because later in the day she was going to Trafalgar Square to a meeting in sympathy with the three-day strike in South Africa in protest against apartheid. She told me which bus to take to her neighborhood, which stop to get off at, and where to meet her. Unfortunately, something went wrong with my watch: it was three-quarters of an hour slow (usually it is fast). I was unaware of this till I got back to my hotel in the evening. I found Susanna frozen at the stop. She must have waited for me a long time, and have cursed me under her breath. She did mutter something about time and lateness, but it did not penetrate to me, because I wasn't aware that my watch was out of order.

Again, it was cold in the house, but in the studio there was a small electric heater. Her pictures were all around. I was impressed by her talent. I liked especially a painting this twenty-six-year-old girl did a few years ago—of a seated, brooding woman with another, a pregnant one, standing against a fence in the background. Her current work was experimental—landscapes, still lifes, hurriedly executed with emphasis on pattern. There was great facility and not enough probing. I told her that she had a dangerous talent, one that makes things come too easily to her, and suggested that she attempt to paint a composition that would be difficult, almost impossible for her to do—with a change of style and technique. She agreed readily, but I think in principle only. "The best advice I ever had," she said in her flippant manner. There was something restless, flighty, uncertain about her. Again, Joseph Herman's words, "We have many good twenty-year-old artists in England, but very few good forty-year-old artists," flashed through my mind.

We went to Trafalgar Square. I listened to the speakers for a while. They sounded so much like the Union Square speakers in the old days. The National Gallery was right there—the temptation was too great. I said good-by to Susanna, after having made a final appointment—this time at my hotel, for tomorrow afternoon, to make a few sketches of her and then to meet Peter, who by that time will be back from Paris, and all have dinner together. The day after, the 31st, I am to fly across the Channel and meet Mary and Arnie in Paris. "Come to my hotel informally dressed, dishevelled, like I saw you the first time at the meeting," I said to Susanna, and added half in jest, "In New York I am known as a painter of dishevelled girls." Before going to bed made a water-color drawing of Henry Moore from memory.

May 30

In the afternoon made sketches of Susanna Bott. She was in an orange pullover and sat against an orange wall in my hotel room. In the evening we met Peter De Francia, had dinner together and parted warmly and exchanged hopes to meet again. Tomorrow am off to Paris.

May 31

In the evening, while registering at the Paris hotel, Mary called that she and Arnie are coming over. Perfect timing. They looked well. We ate somewhere on Boulevard St. Michel, out of doors. They make themselves understood in French, enjoy French food (which always rubs me the wrong way), became wine-drinkers. It was rainy and chilly in Paris (as in London) but we were happy and cozy. Mary and Arnie had already been in the Louvre and at the Musée des Impressionistes, and tomorrow we made arrangements to meet in the Louvre on the top of the stairs near the Victory of Samothrace. "Daddy," Mary said, "you know which painting I really love—I think it is just beautiful . . . Leonardo's 'Madonna of the Rocks' . . . and those portraits by Holbein of the Astronomer, the Bishop, and of Erasmus." Arnie's favorite was that gem by Vermeer, "The Lace Maker."

June 1

We spent the morning in the Louvre. We had lunch somewhere across the bridge and returned to the Louvre to see the "Reserve"

26

collection of countless paintings by David, Ingres, Corot, Delacroix, Géricault and others. It was an exhausting day. Mary and Arnie were patient and understanding. We made an appointment to meet tomorrow afternoon. In the morning Mary and Arnie were going up the Notre Dame to have a close look at the gargoyles and to look down upon Paris. I preferred to go to the Louvre again.

June 2

We had a wonderful afternoon at the Musée des Impressionistes. I expounded to Mary and Arnie about the beauty of the paintings and told some anecdotes I knew about the painters. I love the Fantin-Latour group paintings—the "Hommage à Delacroix" and the two others— the one of Manet surrounded by artists and writers and the one with Verlaine and Rimbaud and with the beautiful still life of flowers. Dégas, of course, is my favorite—his "Absinthe Drinkers" and "Laundresses" are inimitable. At night Mary and Arnie treated me to the opera, *Tosca*. It bored us, but the lavishly baroque interior of the Opera House fascinated us.

June 3

We met in the afternoon again. We had lunch in a Chinese restaurant in the vicinity of the Musée Cluny. Afterwards, Mary and Arnie and I walked about leisurely. We stopped in a few art and book shops. In the evening we bought some bread, cheese, ham and a bottle of wine, and ate below on the steps of the Cité bridge. Some wine was left over, and Mary offered it to a young man who sat a few steps above us. It was accepted matter-of-factly. It was a nice warm evening. The setting of the sun was reflected in the Seine. We went and sat for a while in the beautiful triangular Vert Gallant Park. Young couples were embracing and kissing. Finally, we had to part.

Tomorrow early, Mary and Arnie are going to Italy. Mary admonished me not to do too much flying while in Europe. "Go by train, you don't have to fly all the time." Her eyes and even teeth shone in the dusk. I told them to be careful driving (they will rent a car in Italy), in crossing the streets, and so forth. We kissed. I watched them walk off to their hotel.

June 4

If I were a poet I would compose a poem in praise of the following big paintings in the Louvre:

"Feast at Cana" by Veronese; "Oath of the Horatii," "The Sabine Women" and "Coronation of Napoleon" by David; "Liberty Leading the People" and "The Massacre at Scio" by Delacroix; "The Studio" and "Burial at Ornans" by Courbet.

It was Courbet's "Burial," when I came upon it two years ago, that prompted me to exclaim spontaneously to my wife, "Rebecca, we're kidding ourselves, the best of us are kidding ourselves!" I studied the "Burial" intensively and long this morning: the eloquent and restrained color harmony of black, white, and red, with the brown of the earth and the gray of the sky; the oneness of this color scheme with the content, the composition, the complete absence of melodrama, gesturing and story-telling. And the technique! Who can paint like this today?

Who in the whole world today, including the internationally acclaimed "geniuses" (the contemporary non-objectivists as well as the "prophets" of the many so-called modern movements: Klee, Miro, Mondrian, and the "demi-dieux" themselves, Picasso and Braque), can achieve, say, a "Coronation of Napoleon" or a "Massacre at Scio"? Who today has the will to exert the effort, with the ability to sustain it, necessary to produce masterpieces of such scope and character? Yes we artists are kidding ourselves today. We seem to be playing at being artists. We are like children playing the "Let's Pretend" game. Is profound, thematic, contemplative painting becoming extinct?

I spent this afternoon at the Musée des Impressionistes. I am in love with the three group paintings of artists and writers by Fantin-Latour. There are some early dark still lifes by Cézanne, heavily and gropingly painted, which Arshile Gorky especially loved and imitated in the 1920's. Here, too, are Monet's vigorous paintings from nature in all its aspects, and his last paintings of pond lilies in which the culmination of all his knowledge, observation and love of nature are expressed. What talmudic sophistry and flippant thinking can claim these as the basis for non-objective, expressionistic painting of today, which so completely divorces itself from nature! The Renoir masterpiece "Moulin de la Galette" is on view here—but of course I like Manet and Dégas best. Dégas's "Absinthe Drinkers" has influenced me all my life—modest in size, quiet, almost colorless, aloof, abstract, it is, to me, at any rate, the modern "Giovanni Arnolfini and His Wife." "The Laundresses" is another unique, inimitable painting—influenced by it, I once painted a yawning girl, for which the actress Maureen Stapleton posed.

How modest in size most of the paintings in this Museum are! Van Gogh never painted a large painting. Cézanne, Gauguin, Dégas, Renoir, even Manet and Monet, only occasionally. The group paintings by Fantin-Latour are small canvases when compared to those painted today, especially by non-representationalists. When I look at the magnified non-objective doodles in paint, I think of an article by that charming columnist, Heywood Broun, that was published long ago in the old *World*. I do not any more remember the theme, but it began with a detailed description of a louse (yes, a louse) under a microscope. The insect becomes "formidable like a battleship." It is effective to magnify, and deceptive.

Met Harry Jackson, the sculptor of cowboys, looking with concentration at the Dégas horses. (Wonderful Dégas again! How personal, different, thoughtful, meaningful everything he touched became!) Quite a character, Harry—with his thick reddish-brown beard, shaggy hair, sweet voice, and embroidered cowboy boots. He took out a little package from the pocket of his corduroy jacket, slowly unwrapped it, and we both looked reverently at a tiny Rodin bronze—the head of one of the Citizens of Calais, which he had purchased at the Rodin Museum.

Am looking out of the window in the Orient Express (train) approaching Munich. It is not quite 6 A.M. It is drizzly and seemingly chilly. We pass towns and villages with smoking chimneys, which make me think of the smoking chimneys of Auschwitz.

Munich is a big, unattractive, semi-medieval and semi-modern city. Many wide squares, or rather unnaturally empty spaces. I suspect there were buildings there that were bombed out and their traces and rubble removed. There are many city gates and many churches that resemble armories. In the late afternoon or evening, the city was noisy with traffic, there was a lot of movement and commotion. I watched the hurrying pedestrians. The men were smaller than American men, the women larger than American women. There isn't that contrast in size between men and women as in the States.

I registered, had my continental breakfast, got a taxi, and went to Alte Pinakothek. This building, too, outside and inside, resembles an armory. It is huge, high-ceilinged, cold, uncomfortable, minus the usual lavish baroque decorations. Everything seems made of concrete, the floors, too, and they were hard on my back. The paintings are hung high, many are under glass and stupidly enough there was a lack of benches and chairs to rest on. In an enormous room filled with astonishing paintings by Rubens, there wasn't a chair or a bench. But the museum is filled with great paintings. "The Apostles" and the Christlike self-portrait by Dürer. Holbein and Dürer are the two German painters who rose above their contemporaries. Their work is serene and intense, so unlike the grimacing, contorted, clumsy, naive and at times even comical work of the Cranachs, Altdorfers, Pachers, and others. Even Grünewald is not to my taste. There is an extraordinary painting by Altdorfer though—"The Battle of Alexander"—one of the strangest, minutest-in-detail paintings. There is a group of intense, smallish paintings by Rembrandt illustrating Christ's Passion. They are grippingly realistic. Convincingly realized is the unnatural, miraculous aspect in the paintings—the terrific light that emanates from Christ which dramatically pierces and illuminates the darkness of time and place. There are extraordinary Rubenses. I liked particularly the double portrait of himself and Isabella Brandt, a lovely full-length portrait of Helena Fourment, and one of a shepherd and a nymph, almost like a Rembrandt, so warm and human. Unfortunately, these three paintings were under glass.

There are many Titians and Tintorettos, a troubled Botticelli, "Entombment," three Raphaels even, which I liked immediately without reservations, an unusual thing with me, for I was habitually disappointed in the Raphaels in the Ufizzi, the Pitti and the Vatican. Two years ago I admired only his "Stanze" in the Vatican; the "Madonna di Tempi" is of a woman and child painted with deep insight, and freely, with the discernible brush strokes so dear to artists. I made a drawing of it in pencil, there and then, noted down the approximate colors and went over it in water color in the evening in my room at the hotel.

June 9

Went to Alte Pinakothek again. I discovered a small painting of the Virgin by Antonella da Messina, a portrait, really, of a young, sweet, pious woman with slender hands crossed on her chest, enveloped in a blue shawl against a black background. Am always captivated by the small, dense, cubistic canvases of Da Messina. Also am always affected by color combinations of black and blue in paintings. Made a drawing of it at the Museum, and for the life of me, couldn't get the Virgin's facial expression of almost inane piety; noted down the colors and in the evening colored it. Wanted very much to draw a detail from a Rubens painting, that big female satyr with two horned and bearded baby satyrs sucking at her breasts, her hand lying limply in the genital region of one of the little satyrs, but my back ached from standing on concrete floors in front of paintings and I was tired, so tired in fact that the rest of the afternoon I sat in an interesting park, opposite a huge fountain with a statue of a properly testicled Nordic, with a Buster-Brown haircut and a farm implement over his shoulder, his stance a steal from Michelangelo's David, and some corny horses with water coming out of their nostrils. It was a warm and sunny afternoon. Many young people were sitting around the fountain. I made a drawing of it, and colored it in the evening.

June 10

Came to Vienna in the late afternoon, unpacked and took a long walk. Located the Kunsthistorisches Museum which was already closed for the day, entered parks embellished with lavish baroque monuments to Goethe, Schiller, Mozart and Maria Teresa, religious monuments, fountains, bronze horsemen, galloping horses with naked youths holding them back, and whatnot.

June 11

Spent this morning in the Kunsthistorisches Museum, one of the finest in Europe. Best, well-cleaned and well-preserved examples of European painting beautifully and intelligently hung. A room of portraits by Velásquez. Four portraits of children, three of Margarita Teresa in three stages of early childhood, and a portrait of a little boy. It is difficult to describe them. They are alive, in space, with objects around them. They exist. And yet there is something un-material about them. Is it because they are painted with such infinite and mysterious delicacy? Suffice it to say that Vermeer's "Artist and His Muse" seemed labored and naturalistic in comparison. There are Brueghels, Rubenses, Titians in profusion. Of particular significance for me were three self-portraits of Rembrandt in one of the side, gray-satin-covered alcoves. The "big self-portrait" is three-quarters length, full-face, confident, virile, arms akimbo; the small one—just head and shoulders, also full face, intensely living; the third slightly turned, his brooding forehead and eyes in shadow, cast by the beret. I had for a moment an uncanny feeling that Rembrandt was in the room. There is also that moving early portrait of his old mother with red-rimmed eyes. In a nearby room were Frans Halses. I swiftly stepped out; I couldn't bear them after Rembrandt, they seemed ugly and obstreperous.

June 12

Saw drawings by old masters at the Albertina, famous drawings, often reproduced, by Michelangelo, Raphael, Rubens, Rembrandt, Holbein, Dürer. Quite a collection of Dürer drawings: of his mother, of landscapes and city-scapes, of Apostles, of flowers, of marsh grass, of a bird's wing, of a rabbit. One can truly say of him, "He loved all things both great and small." But the drawing that made my heart melt was the silverpoint of himself at thirteen years of age. Subsequently, Dürer wrote above this drawing that he drew this of himself in the mirror in 1484, "when I was still a child." It was this drawing that I had in mind when in a letter I chided the artist Rudolf Baranik for his being so involved in teaching art to middle-aged amateurs of little or no talent, for giving so much time to them ". . . there is no little Albert Dürer in your class," I remember I wrote to him.

June 13

Studied Brueghel with great attention. I would call his paintings colored drawings—so thinly painted are they, tinted rather than painted, usually on wooden panels. No paint-quality, impasto, "métier," brush strokes; not that his painting is sleek and smooth—it is strangely vigorous, in fact—but its basis is drawing. He was a genre-ist—an unpopular term today, but does it matter? I recalled the argument in Moses Soyer's studio on the eve of my departure for Europe. Joseph Floch and Alex Dobkin were there. It began with Floch's dismissal of some artist's work by calling it genre. I laughingly remarked that everything Floch dislikes he calls genre. And the argument flared up. Moses and Floch insisted that genre is an inferior branch of art. I, supported by Dobkin, maintained that genre can be great—that it depends upon the artist—and mentioned Vermeer, Chardin, Louis Le Nain, Brueghel and Rubens in his "Kermesse." We tried to define genre, we named great and not so great artists and tried to classify them and their work. Now, in the Brueghel room of the Vienna Museum I ruminated: "What is his (Brueghel's) 'Road to Cavalry' if not vast genre in what it encompasses?"

Rubens again overwhelmed me. The three couples of cavorting and prancing nymphs and satyrs in the "Venus Feast" openly and unrestrainedly making love . . . the nymphs voluptuous and as big as the satyrs . . . one satyr embracing his aroused companion's underbelly . . . his hands fumbling in her pubic hair . . .

Went to Belvedere by Strassebahn. Saw a big Cézanne exhibition. There was a strong self-portrait and a variation of his two card players at the table. They were beautiful paintings—generally speaking I like

33

Cézanne's paintings of men better than his still lifes, landscapes and his paintings of women. There was also a silvery study for his big unfinished, unrealized "Bathers"—his "project of doing Poussin over entirely from nature." I remembered this quotation * from the moving letter Cézanne wrote to Emile Bernard shortly before he died, in which he cites the difficulties and obstacles encountered even at the mere contemplation of painting the big canvas from nature, literally from nature —to find the proper setting for the picture "which would not differ from the one I visualized in my mind," to get the many models of men and women willing to undress and motionlessly pose, the difficulties with the out-of-doors weather, and of carrying about so big a canvas. . . . Good old dishevelled Cézanne, how deep and wonderful was his preoccupation with nature!

On the top floor of the Belvedere saw a collection of contemporary Viennese art. I was pleasantly surprised to find a small painting by my friend Joseph Floch. There were two big rooms, one each devoted to Kokoschka and Schiele. A very early—simply beautiful!—painting by Kokoschka, "The Visitation," and a portrait of Oscar Moll, impressed me, but Schiele who died of Spanish influenza at the age of 28 in 1918, was the revelation to me. His three big paintings are there: "A Mother and Two Children," "Death and the Maiden" and "The Family"—of himself, his wife and baby, in reality unborn, for his young, pregnant wife also died of the 'flu—nude, squatting one in front of the other. The first two are masterpieces of a sort. The painting in them is wretched, worried, fussy, the color is spotty—bright and muddy in parts. One feels, however, the terrific effort to master the sticky, messy oily paint. They are works of a young genius. All the morbidity, macabreness and schizophrenia of youth are there. All the storm and stress, the drive and joy of sex and the anguished suppression of it, the wonder and fear of life, and the preoccupation with death. The "family" of himself, his wife and the imaginary, in reality unborn, child, was painted in 1918, the year he died. He was beginning to master the technique of painting then—it is painted with greater ease and fluency, especially the nude figure of his wife. The intensity is about to give way to almost happiness. I liked this painting less. But its content and composition impressed me very much. The figure of himself is well realized, the drawing and painting of the conceived child who was never to be born, touchingly tentative.

* *Artists on Art,* compiled and edited by Robert Goldwater and Marco Treves.

I, too, was stricken by the 1918 influenza and survived. I was eighteen at the time. Surrounded by the Schiele paintings, I recalled to mind and visualized my first one-man exhibition at the Daniel Gallery in New York. I was twenty-nine then, a year older than Schiele was when he died. There were about twelve paintings in all on the gallery walls. I tried to remember them—a few street scenes and still lifes, a portrait of my mother, a family scene, some nudes—all small, withdrawn, restrained. I remembered my then confused state of mind, my social retardation, my fears, my constant suppression of all desires, awareness of my unprepossessiveness, my inarticulateness, etc., etc., also the tensions that came with our large family and the torture of sibling rivalry that never subsided.

. . . What an outburst of self-revealment!

June 18

Back in Paris. Met Rebecca at the Orly Airfield.

June 19

Called up Floch. He came to the hotel. It was nice to see him. In the afternoon he took us to the studio of Joseph Constant, a Parisian sculptor of animals, a whimsical, gray-haired man, vaguely resembling Charlie Chaplin. Both he and his wife emigrated to Paris from Russia after the First World War. They speak Russian beautifully. We liked his animals in wood, terra cotta, and bronze. We purchased a kitten—we thought it would make a good present for Mary and Arnie. Constant was pleased. He fondled the bronze kitten as if it were a live one, firmly and tenderly, with a big and masculine hand, talking the while with charming Russian intonation. "It is a young one, still blind. Look, his eyes are just about ready to open," etc. His wife is a good painter of portraits and still lifes.

Rebecca and I spent this morning in the Louvre and looked at the Flemish paintings. The small "Madonna of Chancellor Rolin" by Van Eyck is in wonderful condition. It is indestructible. It was painted, if I remember correctly, in 1436—525 years ago. It was not merely painted, it was architected, molded . . . and painted . . . jewelled and brocaded. We looked long at the Avignon "Pieta." This is what Rebecca wrote to a friend about it: "Hanging alone in a small alcove, it is almost a shrine for those who believe that painting is one means of communicating deep human emotions in a tangible representational manner, universally understood. And it is permeated by an aesthetic quality that none of our barren practitioners in contemporary abstraction can hope to attain."

The Louvre is exciting and noisy. It is ten museums in one. There is a continuous and restless quest for Mona Lisa, Venus de Milo, the Victory, and loud exclamations of awe and admiration in front of them. The clatter of shoe-clad feet, the sharp click-clack of women's high heels, especially, on the wooden floors, the sound of countless voices of the herds of men and women following the loudly expounding guides, create a veritable cascade of noise.

Saw the Chagall exhibition of stained glass windows for an Israeli synagogue exhibited in a specially erected pavilion in proximity to the Louvre. Typically Chagall—in color and symbols—twelve windows in all, for each of the twelve tribes. We liked them, Rebecca especially, due, I think, to her interest in history. In the evening we went with Joseph [Floch] to the opening of a very comprehensive retrospective exhibition of Maillol, his sculpture, paintings, drawings, prints—his life's work. It was an impressive and beautiful show. That such serenity existed in our epoch of wars and social and political upheavals and all sorts of cultural confusions is sort of miraculous.

Met the sculptor Ossip Zadkine at the exhibition, a small, thin, handsome, snappy man, with pink complexion and snow-white hair and eyebrows; gives one a sense of vitality and versatility. Speaks English well—he lived in New York during the Second World War and taught sculpture at the Art Students' League.

June 24

Visited Ossip Zadkine in his studio in a private little copse in a courtyard in the heart of Montparnasse. There are a few studios and living quarters on the premises where he and his wife, the painter Valentine Prax, live and work. I asked Mr. Zadkine to pose for a drawing. He sat down without much ado. I liked him a lot. Some of his work, too—his imaginative and poetic versions of "Poet," "Orpheus," etc., the tragic feeling in his war themes. Vital, spirited, moving work. He just completed a monument to Van Gogh which will be unveiled in a week (he invited my wife and me to the ceremonies of the unveiling but we will have left Paris by then) about 50 kilometers from the city, in the square opposite a little church that Van Gogh immortalized in one of his paintings. He showed me two tragic, Rodin-like, manly heads of the one-eared Van Gogh—studies for the monument. Zadkine seems to me becoming more figurative in his work. We conversed in Russian, one of the several languages he speaks well. I mentioned his international fame and his ready retort was that fame is nothing—that a man is no greater or smaller than he is. He asked me about an artist who has been living and working in New York these many years. I said that materially he is successful, but that morally he has lost ground. Well, Zadkine said, this man always impressed him as carrying a fear within himself, but that he was unable to do anything with this fear, to artistically exploit it. Some artists, he said, were able to do this, and their work was enhanced. He cited Otto Dix as an example. I was impressed by his mentioning the comparatively little-known Dix,* whose work, when I come upon it, invariably impresses me.

In the evening we met the Detroit art dealer Bob Garelick who had stopped in Paris on his way home from Germany and Italy. For the second time today Otto Dix was mentioned in conversation. Garelick showed me European art publications and catalogues among which was

---

* There is a very interesting article on Otto Dix, written by Alfred Barr, that appeared in an art magazine many years ago. I was so impressed by it I saved it.

a paper-backed book of reproductions of Dix's work, some in color. Upon seeing the deep interest I evinced in Dix, Garelick presented it to me.

Mr. Garelick talked with his customary enthusiasm about contemporary art in East Germany and in Italy. He told me that he'll put on an exhibition of representational Italian sculpture and painting and call it "The New Renaissance of Italian Art," or "The New Renaissance of Figurative Italian Art," his aim being, he told me, to counter the many officially and popularly encouraged non-figurative exhibitions that prevail today, and to impress upon the public that good figurative art is being created, that artists are returning to representationalism. As always, he oversimplified things and spoke with his habitual lack of restraint. Irritated, I advised him to desist from using words and phrases like "Renaissance" and "New Renaissance," that the figurative painting that is being done at this moment should be subjected to strict scrutiny and criticism before it is acclaimed. I was, however, for putting on, if at all possible, high-level exhibitions of figurative art, and if it is to be of Italian art, I suggested titles like "Contemporary Representational Italian Painting and Sculpture" or "Representational Painting and Sculpture in Italy Today," or even, "Re-emergence of Representational Art in Italy." I am skeptical about Italian art of the moment, especially about painting. Only one of the younger Italian painters impresses me: Guttuso. Sculpture fares better in Italy—but certainly the outstanding ones are only Manzu and the early Marino Marini; there are others, gifted but inferior.

June 25

Rebecca and I visited the young American painter John Dobbs and his wife, and had dinner at their house. We saw his year's work, done in Paris. It is talented, impetuous, uncertain as yet. But he made progress. Plans to live and work in Paris for some years, and in a year to have an exhibition there. There is some logic in young artists wanting to exhibit and gain recognition in both America and Europe, and even wanting to work in more than one country or continent. And yet great art was always local. Degas wrote from America, where he visited and painted for a brief period, that he needed his Paris in order to create. "I want only my own corner and devote myself to it fully." I always liked an aphorism that I have encountered somewhere in my reading, and I think the author of it was Derain: "Stupidity is national, intelligence is international, and *art is local.*" However, the world is getting smaller all the time, and the phrase "art is local" is beginning to lose its meaning.

June 26

Joseph Floch took me to Mrs. Kars, widow of the painter who committed suicide during the Nazi occupation of Paris. Kars was in the circle of Pascin, Utrillo, Valadon, Soutine and others. She is old and florid, her big face lavender with powder. On the walls hang a portrait of her in her youth by Valadon, Kars's self-portrait, and a fine early figure painting by Pascin. She has many drawings by and mementos of Modigliani, Pascin, Kandinsky, Picasso, Juan Gris, and others—quite a valuable (artistically and money-wise) collection. She was disturbed this morning, and understandably so, because (she told us) a dealer came to see her the evening before in the hopes of acquiring part of her collection, and insensitively hinted at her age, the proximity and inevitability of death. He said, "Well, Mrs. Kars, now that you will soon have to prepare yourself for the long, long journey, what are the plans for your collection?"

June 28

There is a feeling of corruption in the contemporary art atmosphere of Paris. Galleries are rented by artists for their exhibitions, art critics literally sell themselves and accept money from artists and galleries for mentioning them and criticizing them favorably in their art columns. Clever, superficial, even mediocre art is taken for granted, is accepted, and no one pays particular attention to it.

Went to the Rodin Museum with Floch. In the garden was an international exhibition of sculpture. Emilio Greco, the Italian sculptor, was featured. He was represented by a number of sculpture pieces and drawings. There was a repetitiousness about his work, both in content and technique. We saw some banal representational pieces by sculptors from a socialist country; absurd American, British and French non-objective contraptions, devoid of meaning and aesthetics; and some of the "New Images of Man" variety of sculpture of big-bellied, spindle-legged or legless figures with testicles as if eaten away by rats, with faceless physiognomies; sculpture, in short, that revels in death, decomposition, necrophilia.

We went inside the Rodin Museum and looked at and studied his well-known pieces, the plaster casts of his countless studies for them, and his inimitable drawings so thoroughly pulsating with life. "You know," said Floch musingly, "it seems to me that so much that's wonderful, deep and profound has already been explored by man, and expressed in art, but there is still room in art for nonsense and exasperating foolishness. What we saw in the garden will not subside so soon. Absurdity in art may continue for a long time yet."

Spent two days in Basle, two mornings in the Fine Arts Museum, which is divided into two parts—on the upper floor is the display of the more recent painting beginning with Cézanne, while the old masters are shown on the lower floor. To me, Holbein's portrait of his wife and children is the finest painting in the entire museum. Mentally I compared it to Rubens's gay, warmly humorous and colorful portrayal of his family in the Louvre. As a matter of fact, many artists have painted variations on this theme—Holbein's is the least sentimental and the least adorned. How powerfully modelled are the heavy-featured faces of the sad mother and the two disturbed children. The background is a dark green, without any suggestion of place or space.

Upstairs is the so-called modern section (how I dislike to use the word "modern" in relation to art!), too systematically, too neatly arranged;

there are, however, some fine examples of early Picasso, one—a favorite with me—of a nude boy carrying a younger child on his back, and Kokoschka's "Tempest"—perhaps too poetic in idea and color. I was impressed this time by some Corinths and, to a lesser extent, by some Hodlers. In a dark room on the ground floor I found Otto Dix's portrait of his parents, perhaps too deliberately crude and objective a painting. I liked it.

July 6

Arrived in Milan at 6 P.M. after a six-hour train ride through the panoramic Alps scenery. Milan is noisy, big, bustling. Subway digging is going on all around the Cathedral.

July 7

Went to Brera in the morning. Among many run-of-the-mill Italian *seicento* paintings, saw Mantegna's foreshortened dead Christ, a good Tintoretto of the "St. Mark" series, the early Raphael, "Marriage of the Virgin," and the very beautiful Piero della Francesca of a "Madonna and Child surrounded by Saints." The Raphael and the Piero are in a separate alcove of a room and the visitors are routed to them after seeing all the other paintings. The guard in that room was proud of the two paintings in his care, and seeing how interested we were in them, asked which of the two pleased us more. He was gratified when we pointed to the Piero della Francesco and informed us that he, too, preferred it to the Raphael. Of course, he said, Raphael is a great name, but look—and he gestured to the Piero—at the *"perspettiva,"* the *"architettura,"* the composition, and the faces of the Saints, one of them—he singled out a figure—is an *"autoritratto."*

In the late afternoon we went to the Colonna Gallery which is run by Madame Usiglio, whom Peter De Francia from London advised me to see, since she is in contact with contemporary Italian artists. She was very helpful, gave us names and addresses of artists, to visit in Florence,

41

Rome and Venice. While there, made an appointment with the Milanese artist Pino Ponti, who happened to come into the gallery just then, to visit him in his studio tomorrow morning.

July 8

Rebecca and I spent an interesting morning with Pino Ponti in his studio. Ponti, a wiry man with warm, swift eyes, was friendly, animated and articulate. He showed us his paintings and drawings—completely representational work. His theme is young women, singly or in groups, usually in street clothes, handbag hanging from the wrist, black or red hair slightly dishevelled or tousled, often smiling, parted lips showing teeth. Inwardly I criticized the similarity of their faces and bodies and the prevailing mood about them of sweet morbidity. He had a painting called "Anne Frank," which impressed me more. It was painted with greater vigor and, strangely enough, seemed less romantic. And frankly I was impressed with the idea: now, why hadn't it ever occurred to me to paint an Anne Frank? I asked myself. Goodness knows, I painted many girls who could have evoked the wonderful Anne Frank.

He showed some of his landscapes, too, city-scapes, rather, of weather-tempered and time-patinated facades of Italian houses. In a sense I liked them more than his figure paintings—they were less showy.

He willingly agreed to pose for a sketch. We conversed the while—that is, my wife translated the questions I asked him in her "petit peu" French and his answers into English. His French wasn't too good but the three of us understood one another. I wanted to know what kind of relationship the artists in Italy have with one another, about artists' organizations or groups, exhibitions, etc. Since I am so impressed by Guttuso and so eager to meet him I asked what he thought about him. Well, his answers to my questions were negative: there is no such thing as close artists' relationship, as a matter of fact there is not much love lost among them, because there is too much competition for economic and artistic status, for attention recognition, prizes and sales. Guttuso, he said, as an artist is too propagandistic, as a man too ambitious, that his following is among the younger artists, who expect favors from him, for he is very influential in the official artistic circles and serves often on prize-awarding art juries.

After lunch went to a small church where Leonardo's "Last Supper" is found. We were impressed nay, amazed to see how much beauty and strength this semi-ruined mural still retains. How durable these masterpieces are—the Sistine Chapel, the Carmine Masaccios and this Leonardo, how indestructible. For centuries they had been neglected in dank churches, blackened and discolored by dust and candle smoke, cracking, peeling, repeatedly repainted and restored and otherwise mistreated. Yet enough beauty and life still emanate from them to make nations wonder.

While writing the above saw my reflection in the mirror, the reflection of the hotel room with Rebecca asleep on the cot; the scene was so hotel-like and dreary—quietly not to awaken Rebecca I got my sketchbook out of the suitcase and made a drawing.

July 9

Set out 9 A.M. in the morning in a bus for Venice with stops and guided tours at Verona, Vicenza and Padua, which needless to say proved unsatisfactory, for the stops were brief, the guides mediocre. But we did get an inkling of the beauty of Verona, of its squares and courtyards. In Padua we stopped on the big square, where we admired the Strozzi monument by Donatello. The Church of St. Anthony appeared huge and clumsy and its interior glitter and clutter repelled us. There was no time to see the great Padua Giottos; we considered ourselves lucky that we saw and admired them two years ago.

July 12

We spent four full days in Venice. Saw the sumptuous Venetian paintings in the Accademia, the Scuola Tintorettos, and the Carpaccios in the Accademia, and his murals in a little church in a very picturesque section of Venice. One day while waiting for a church to open, where there are some splendid Tintorettos, we sat down somewhere in the shade. I made a drawing of a deserted street—it was still siesta time, the

43

afternoon was wonderful and crystalline, the street was half in shade and half in light; the ancient walls of the buildings were almost as luminous in the shade as they were in the light. Rebecca was busy the while, both writing a letter and paying heed to a little girl and pretending to understand the chatter addressed to her. The child had a red balloon attached to a string; she held it in one hand and kept pointing to it with her other hand. She spoke with animation and expressive gestures, little Italian that she was, for some time, but suddenly realizing that something was amiss for no response was forthcoming from Rebecca, abruptly ended her monologue, shrugged her shoulders and walked off.

We spent a good deal of time with a New York acquaintance, the painter Enid Smiley who has been coming to Venice for many years. We were introduced by her to the charming restaurant "Montin" frequented by writers, intellectuals and artists. Through her we met a few Venetian artists, one of them being Cadorin, the Director of the Accademia Art School, a man in his late sixties, tall, heavy, pink, with the distinguished features of a Roman Senator. We visited him in his studio. He dressed himself up for the occasion in some kind of a Chinese robe of heavy material with wide silver-embroidered sleeves— a fancy smock, I guessed. The gradually increasing mid-day heat forced him to shed the robe after a while. He asked us to sit down (there were other visitors—Claire Hooton, the Lishinskys, New York artists, and Enid) and ceremoniously began to show his paintings, setting them up one by one on a tremendous easel that must have been centuries old. There was something ceremonious also about his paintings—static and dignified—painted thickly and smoothly, smoothly plastered rather than painted, chalky in color. There was something not quite right about the paintings—they were like strange fruit that one wouldn't eat and yet would hate to throw out. I made a quick sketch of him with Claire Hooton in the background. He posed immobile as a statue.

Venice is beautiful this year. Every inch of it is beautiful. The weather is pleasanter than two years ago. It seems also quieter. San Marco is dimmer at night, there seem to be fewer tourists than two years ago and as then a good percentage of them are leather-hosed, camera-laden, arrogant Germans.

The nearer we approached Florence the more beautiful the landscape became and the more familiar, for the terraced hills, the olive trees, the hill towns recalled to us the backgrounds in the paintings of Mantegna, Piero della Francesca, Botticelli and others. Half an hour after we registered in the hotel we were in the Uffizi—it was a joy to behold again the Filippino Lippis, the Botticellis, Titian's "Venus of Urbino," Raphael's "Pope Leo," and above all, Hugo van der Goes's "Portinari Altarpiece." Later we walked up and down Ponte Vecchio, sat down in an out-of-doors cafe in Piazza Signoria, ordered drinks, felt at peace and at home, watched the tourists, the natives, and the children feeding the forever gluttonous and defecating pigeons.

"Daddy, you were right, Florence is a golden city," wrote Mary to us from Italy. It seemed even lovelier this time than two years ago. Again we began our round of visits to museums, churches, palazzos, etc. Met the Rabins. Bernie, knowing of my desire to meet some of the local artists, said he will contact one Grazzini, whom he knew when he was here a few years ago, and arrange for a visit.

We couldn't find the Alexanders in the phone book (Sidney Alexander—poet and author of *Michelangelo the Florentine*, the first volume of his projected trilogy), so we decided to walk over to his house, and much to our delight we remembered the way to Porta Romana and up the hill to via Ugo Foscolo where the Alexanders live. We climbed up the four or five "pianos" only to find them out, and be greeted by Arno, their terrier. My wife left a note with the maid.

Went to the Duomo to see Michelangelo's "Pieta." I sketched it hurriedly two years ago. Will try to make a more elaborate drawing of it this time. The head of St. Nicodemus is sculpted broadly, the way Rembrant painted at the end of his life. The figure of Mary too is wonderful. They are not the proud disdainful figures of Michelangelo's youth —they are compassionate and sorrowful. The St. Nicodemus, Michelangelo's self-portrait, is as full of humility and resignation to life and death as Rembrandt's "St. Paul" in the Ryksmuseum, which also is a self-portrait.

July 16

Mrs. Alexander called us and invited us to a cocktail party, the day after tomorrow.

Have been to the Uffizi every single morning. This afternoon we went in quest of the Castagno mural the "Last Supper." When after some wanderings and circling about the neighborhood we found the former monastery where the mural was painted, we didn't know the entrance to it and a passerby had to show us the door and point to an almost invisible bell button to press. A tall ascetic-looking Italian let us in and proudly directed us to the fresco, and in basic Italian, understandable even to us, told us, that it had been cleaned, simply washed with water, that no restoration of any kind was needed, it was well preserved under the centuries' accumulation of dust and dirt, but that the interior of the building itself is in the process of restoration, which was evident to us from the bags of cement and the bricks on the floor. The Castagno is strong, decorative and non-emotional. The design of the composition and of each individual figure is powerful and expressive. The figure of Judas is particularly striking—shaggy, dark, sinister, distinct.

On the way back we found ourselves at a street where we knew Mimi Gross, daughter of sculptor Chaim Gross, had been living and painting for a year and a half. We decided to look her up there and then. We found the number of her house, wended our way through a courtyard, onto which several gaping doors opened. We found Mimi's name among others on a mailbox, with an arrow pointing to the left. Up one flight we met someone who directed us to a door in a long corridor of doors. This led out to an open empty terrace, at the other end of which was a partly open door, decorated gaily, childishly, with painted clowns, animals, flowers; that of course was it. We knocked; there being no response we peeped in and beheld a mass of color on the walls (paintings, reproductions) and a mess of clothes, bundles, palettes, etc. on the floor. We left a note for Mimi to call us.

July 18

Came back from Pitti Palace. Impressed this time by some of the Raphaels. But they and other great paintings are poorly displayed and submerged in the great number of third- and fourth-rate old master paintings: the Dolcis, Del Sartos, the Guido Renis, etc.

In the hotel lobby we found Mimi and her friend Red Grooms waiting for us. Mimi, chubby, dishevelled, the eyelids of her warm, brown, inward-looking eyes painted blue. Red, a cross between Li'l Abner and Bergman's *Seventh Seal* knight—tall, hungry-looking, sharp-elbowed, red-haired. They were dressed beatnik-ly, bizarrely, sloppily. Mimi was genuinely happy to see us; Red, shyly so. We told them of our date this afternoon (at the Alexanders') and that we would love to meet them tomorrow in their studios (same building), see their work, and have dinner together.

The Rabins, too, were invited to the Alexanders' and we went together. The party was dull, the conversation lagged. But we admired the panoramic view from the veranda of the city with its overpowering Duomo, its church spires and towers, and its hilly outskirts. The Alexanders who love their Florence would from time to time call their guests' attention to its beauty and its soft light. We had a few drinks and left early. I told Sidney that I would like to sketch him before we left for Rome next week.

July 19

The Rabins took us to visit Grazzini, a Florentine artist of some reputation. On the way we stopped into Santa Croce and saw some fragments of Giotto's murals on freshly replastered walls. Rabin, who

47

is a restorer by profession, explained to us that later repaintings of and additions to the murals had been scraped or washed off and only what was genuinely by Giotto is left. These fragments of groups of heads, or say, of a single kneeling figure, float disconnectedly and surrealistically in the expanses of fresh plaster.

Grazzini, a pleasant, smallish, disarming man, had his young son in the studio. Theirs is a warm father-and-son relationship. Grazzini told us with restrained emotion that his son's young comrade, a schoolmate, had died from leukemia that morning. He shook his head from side to side, and gently patted the boy on the back; the boy also shook his head in thoughtful resignation. Grazzini then showed us his paintings and drawings. They were good, or rather, not bad. They were too sketchy for me, not conclusive, but did in some way reflect the genuineness and modesty of the man. He, too, told us that there was not much friendliness and socializing among artists in Florence and in Italy generally; that they work in isolation; that he and Guttuso are of the same generation, that they were friends once. "But I don't see him now, As a matter of fact, it is easier for you American artists to get to Guttuso than for us Italian artists." There was a note of bitterness in his voice. It is becoming apparent to me that a very small group of Italian artists have far outstripped their contemporaries in achievement and fame.

In the afternoon went to Mimi and Red. They have adjoining studios. Mimi's studio was orderly, neatly swept that morning, sunny and cheerful. On the walls hung her exuberant, completely uninhibited paintings. She told me in her low—as if talking to herself—voice, that she likes German expressionism and is influenced by it. I readily saw this. Her work certainly is expressionistic, with abandon, childishly, uninhibitedly, unself-critically so. On the walls, besides her own paintings, hung many reproductions of Sienese paintings, interesting photographs, carved and gaily painted Sicilian donkey cart slats, Mexican votive pictures, etc.

Red's studio was austere in comparison, less cluttered; his work, too, less gay and colorful, but sensitive.

It was still too early for dinner so I asked them to pose for me which they did, sitting next to one another. Mimi was attired tightly in red and brown, her hair like Medusa's; Red Grooms in a turtle-neck mustard-yellow sweater which, with his red hair, created a strange harmony, or rather combination of colors. There was a large canvas on the floor beside them. Mimi called my attention to it. It was recklessly painted and raucous in color. "I had the 'Jewish Bride' by Rembrandt in

48

mind," she said, looking at me with her soft brown eyes that at the same time seemed to be looking stubbornly into herself, "when I painted this of me and Red."

"What a travesty," I said to myself, and smiled to her as one does to a child.

While posing Mimi talked incessantly, telling about her travels with Grooms all over Europe and the Near East, their experiences, amusing and difficult ones, their occasional financial crises, etc. They were both pleased with the drawing I made of them. "I like the way you made me," Mimi said simply.

The time had come to go out to dinner. Mimi, for some reason, suggested one of the swankiest Florentine restaurants. We ate well, but we were under constant scrutiny. The fashionable diners and formal waiters looked at Mimi and Grooms with frank amazement. I suddenly noticed that the legitimate split on the side of Mimi's skirt was enlarged by a rent, and her thigh, which was covered with oil paint smudges, exposed itself every time she moved or gestured. Both Mimi and Grooms, who resembled a parrot with his red hair and yellow sweater, were aware of the sensation they caused and bravely tried to ignore the diners and the waiters but once in a while cast angry and moody glances in their direction.

They told us that they were living these summer weeks outside Florence in a villa on a farm with other young artists, poets, musicians, communally, all guests of a young art historian whom they call "captain" because he always wears a hat with a visor and who at this time is in Rome, doing research for his M.A. thesis on the work of, "Guess who?" Mimi said to me in derision. "Guido Reni! As if there are no other artists to write about!"

I couldn't more heartily agree with her. Mimi said she would call us in a day or two and invite us to spend an afternoon and evening at the villa. "It is on a farm. There are many animals there, horses, cows, dogs, ducks." Mimi's eyes glowed with love and pleasure. "The villa is on a hill, we have a wonderful view of Florence." She mentioned a few times a particular horse that was left in her charge, and a carriage— "a surrey with a fringe on top," which she was decorating at the moment (hence the painted thigh, I thought). She said something about traveling with Grooms all the way to Verona with this horse and carriage, with some kind of puppet or movie show.

It was late when we walked home. How small European cities seem to me! How every place is within walking distance! As now, we walked

49

through almost half of Florence to get to our hotel, and it wasn't tiring. It was interesting to pass churches and palazzos, to cross piazzas and wind ourselves through narrow, smelly, ill-lit alleys unchanged since Cellini's time.

July 20

The Van der Goes "Portinari Altarpiece" makes the Lorenzo Credis, the Ghirlandaios and even the Filippino Lippis in the room look positively insipid. Every time I look at it I discover something new and wonderful—the differences in scale of the figures, the moody angels—some strangely still, some fluttering about like bats—the animated shepherds, the portraits of the Portinaris, the fascinating and meaningful still life of wheat and flowers at the bottom of the central panel.

There is insane poetry in Botticelli's "Spring" and in his moody religious compositions. One of the most interesting paintings to me in the whole of the Uffizzi is his "Adoration of the Magi." It is like a Flemish painting in its beauty of detail and in that many of the figures are portraits. Only the Botticelli is mellow in color, and the figures, at least, in this painting are relaxed, fancifully attired, debonair—unlike their severely draped pious, Flemish counterparts whose hands are always folded in prayer, fear and supplication.

Red Grooms and his friend, Paul Suttman, a shaggy, red-bearded giant, called to take us to their villa. We all piled into Paul's small car, where huddled was also Paul's wife, Gwynne, a tall stringy girl with very delicate features. Distances are small in Italy, and in no time we were on the farm where their villa was on top of the hill. Mimi, shining with welcome, descended some stairs and approached and kissed us. Her hair was wet, she just took a bath, she told us, and began taking us around. She introduced us to the inhabitants of the villa—Natasha, a lovely girl of quiet mien, a poetess, born in Paris of Russian parents, lived and went to school in the States for the duration of the war and at present a student of literature on a fellowship in Oxford University, England; Peter, a young bearded folk singer with the naïve face of a Saint. (Rebecca was taken by the beauty of his eyes, his whole being, she said, seemed to breathe music.). Mimi reintroduced us to the Suttmans; Paul, a sculptor who studied with Manzu and served as a model for his

50

teacher's "Caravaggio" of all things—this tall, shaggy, buck-toothed American—and Gwynne, his wife, a painter, tall, thin-armed, with a cameo-like face. Needless to say, they were all informally dressed, in shorts, or tight, faded, patched jeans, except for Natasha, who was in a neat summer dress. The quiet air about her was almost tangible. Mimi took us around the farm and introduced us to the farmers—men with open, tanned, sun-wrinkled, wine-loving faces. They looked with tolerant amusement upon Mimi and us, laughed readily and pointed out to us the beauty of the "panorama."

We saw and expressed our admiration for the carriage, every bit of which Mimi had vividly and gaily decorated. There were farm animals, cows, ducks, geese, prowling cats and frolicking dogs, and there was Mimi's big horse, around whom we all gathered in great concern of what to do about the millions of flies that buzzed and hovered about him, clung to his flanks and head, around his big shiny eyes especially—"maybe to tape his eyes for a few minutes and spray him with some insect repellent?" Rebecca, as always interested in the trees, flowers, plants of a place, would break off a small twig, pluck a leaf or a flower, examine it, and give it its name. Two little Australian sisters appeared on the scene, shy at first, but friendly and boisterous after a while. The smaller of them went off suddenly and came back with a posy of field flowers and offered it to Rebecca with the words, "Flowers for the lady visitor." All around us were hills, some with towns perched on them, their sides terraced with cultivated patches. Below lay peaceful valleys. Close by, a tenant farmer with a team of white oxen plowed his portion of the field and far beyond him was the beautiful silhouette of Florence.

Finally we entered the house and found ourselves in a tremendously large, high-ceilinged bare room with paintings and prints on the walls, books and magazines strewn about. I was shown an issue of *Art News* with an article by Alan Kaprow called "Happenings on the New York Scene," about a group of young artists, "who are translating painting into a new kind of Drama." I had no time to read the article, but I glanced at it. Well, I guess one can make of it what one wants . . . the big thing was that there was a picture of Red Grooms in the magazine, creating, or acting in, one of the "Happenings." Also an issue of *Life* was lying around opened to an illustrated article on Kokoschka's school at Salzburg. This was where the Suttmans and Mimi Gross and Red Grooms studied sculpture and painting last year, met and became friends. Manzu was the sculpture instructor there and seeing for the

51

first time the tall, red-bearded, shaggy American, exclaimed, "Caravaggio," and asked him to pose. Red's, Mimi's and Gwynne's opinion of Kokoschka was not a flattering one because (I suspect) he didn't make much of them and these kids, independent and full of bravado though they seem to be on the surface, are really as insecure as orphans are and crave attention and approval.

The lights were turned on. The little Australian girls went off to sleep. We sat around the table subdued and silent, waiting for dinner. Presently, at the quiet order of Natasha the clean tablecloth was spread and enormous amounts of meat, spaghetti, salad, and bread, and jugs of wine appeared on the table. Our contribution was a huge *panetone*— a sort of coffee cake stuffed with nuts and fruit. Two strangers—Italian men—wandered in out of the night. The food was gone and they were offered wine. There prevailed a mood of relaxation and quiet merriment. Rebecca and I were moved by the friendliness these young people had shown us. One of the Italians, after a consultation with his friend, pointed to Rebecca and said that he wanted to sing a song to "Mama." The song was long and sentimental and was accompanied by the singer's histrionic gestures and pious eye-rolling at her.

We left the table finally, and sat in front of a lighted screen, in darkness, and the invisible Grooms proceeded to show his, and Mimi's, shadowgraph movie to the music accompaniment of the also invisible Peter. The main character was a Don Quixote figure on a horse, and whenever he jogged across the screen, one of the Italians would joyfully exclaim: "Cowboy *stanco!*"—tired cowboy, which for some reason amused Rebecca and she would go off into peals of laughter. It was getting late and we were beginning to be tired. Our amusement became tempered by the pensive awareness of how young our hosts were, of our own age, of flight of time, etc. Before we left, we invited this lovable gang of fellows and girls to dinner, some evening soon, in a restaurant of their choosing. "Caravaggio" Suttman took us home.

July 23

In the late afternoon Paul called for us at the hotel and drove us to his studio. We were to meet Mimi and Red and drive to the restaurant where the others would be. The studio was in Via Degli Artisti, a little tree-shaded alley of a street. There was a row of studios. A young sculptor was busy casting in front of his doorway, his pretty wife with a baby in her arms, watching him. Everything was so damn idyllic! The Suttman place was high-ceilinged, square, bare of furniture except for a couple of taborets, a cot, a table, Gwynne's frameless paintings and drawings on the whitewashed walls, Paul's small scuptures, in the style of Madordo Rossi (a sculptor who died in the twenties, I think, and whose work at present is in vogue) on the window sill. There was a disorderly kitchen with the inevitable bundles of clothes, rags, palettes and brushes on the floor, probably because of lack of closet space. We had tea, after which I sketched Paul and Gwynne. I expressed the hope of meeting Manzu, the Italian sculptor I like most, when we will be in Rome in a week or so, but Suttman dispelled it by telling me that by that time Manzu will have left Rome for somewhere near Bergamo, where he (Suttman) is to join him in a few days and together make a pilgrimage to Madordo Rossi's home where the bulk of his work is kept. There were some vague intimations that we might join them.

Soon we heard a motorcycle come to a halt in the alley. Mimi and Red came in, in a hurry. Mimi's glance hurriedly swept over the paintings on the wall and she perfunctorily exclaimed: "Gwynnie, it's terrific." The five of us piled into the Suttman car, all except Red who went on his motorcycle to get Peter and his guitar, and directed by Mimi, we drove in the direction of Piazza Michelangelo on the other side of the Arno, and we soon got to Beppo's restaurant.

We were seated out-of-doors under trees around a long table laden with food, wine and fruit. Peter sang American folk songs and accompanied himself on the guitar and often we all joined in the chorus, as did the diners at other tables. There were newcomers with us whom we had not met before—a young Italian novelist and his American girl friend and translator. Red pulled out a huge sketchbook and began to draw Rebecca, energetically, stretching his neck out from across the table and peering at her at close range. Later I too tried to draw this group of festive young people—Peter, his smooth-complexioned head bobbing up and down making music on his guitar, songs pouring out of his open mouth; Paul, with his flaming beard and bucktoothed smile, and Red Grooms in an outlandish jacket also red, with sleeves too short for him; the handsome Italian novelist, and all the sweet girls. But I had too much wine and my pencil wobbled and fumbled over the white sheet, as I was drawing the profile of the Italian novelist's girl, nearest to me, with the moon in the black sky, partly veiled by a small trans-

53

parent cloud, resting lightly on her head, barely touching her hair. "You have a beautiful hat on," I said. "It consists of the round moon and a small transparent cloud."

July 24

Siena is sinister, medieval, stony, hilly. It was hot with an oppressive, before-a-storm heat, and for the first time in Europe my head ached as if I were sunstruck. Rebecca, more alertly than I, responded to the strange beauty of Siena and was impressed by the shell-shaped main square. We went into the museum and saw the Sienese paintings, among which is beautifully displayed Duccio's big altarpiece of the enthroned Madonna surrounded by Saints—his masterpiece. Frankly, early Italian paintings never interested me very much. They are icons really, not paintings. For me Italian art begins with Masaccio, Filippino Lippi, Botticelli, etc. I was glad, however, that these paintings are in the museum. So well displayed and no longer in the churches for which they were painted. I wish all paintings, and wherever possible frescoes, were transferred from the dank churches, where they are either in complete darkness or cheaply illuminated by floodlights. How good it would be, for instance, to get the magnificent St. Matthew paintings of Caravaggio from the church of S. Luigi dei Francesi and hang them on a museum wall in good light.

July 25

At the American Consulate we were given the address and telephone of Kenneth Tilkemeyer, a former student of mine, who married an Italian girl artist, and is settled or getting settled in Florence. Ken called for us this morning—there was one of those sudden, unexpected, unpublicized bus strikes in Florence and since he has no car, he walked, ran, rather, he told us, to be at our hotel at the appointed time. On the way to his house we stepped into the church, Santa Maria del Carmine, at my request, to take another look at the Masaccios. Well, again, I was

54

deeply moved by them. I heard Ken saying rapidly under his breath, as is his wont, that nobody paints like this any more and therefore there is no point to do so. "You know, Ken," I said with deliberate slowness, "if I were a young man today, like you, this is how I would choose to try to paint, like Masaccio, unaffectedly, strongly, truthfully. I wouldn't give a damn about all the weird, ephemeral art movements of the moment, fashionable, publicized and encouraged though they may be."

It was nice at the Tilkemeyers. His Italian wife is charming, a graphic artist of talent, their little daughter lovely. Ken's intention—it may not be conscious on his part—is to become thoroughly Italian both in life as well as in art. He signs his paintings "Tilke."

We ate delicious spaghetti, and drank *grappa*, a strong alcoholic drink, something like vodka. Later we went down to his studio and he showed us his work. He had not as yet accomplished much. Unfortunately he seems to have fallen under the influence of the late Italian artist, Ottone Rosai, whom he came to know through his wife. She studied with Rosai who, she told me, was her "second father." He died several years ago and is being made much of today. A big, lush monograph on his work was just published in Florence, his paintings are avidly sought after and command high prices. I don't like his work, it is soft and bone- less. Occasionally there is a morbid quality in some of his paintings which intrigues me. But he certainly is not a master, and not a fortunate example for a young man to emulate. As it was, Ken's work seemed soft, careless and weak. He has talent, though. I criticized him, too gently, I am afraid. But I did advise him to intensify his drawing and color and work long on his paintings, not to consider them finished, when they are mere beginnings, in fact.

July 26

We came to the Alexanders' about 5 P.M. Had drinks, and for the second time admired the view from the terrace. Golden and luminous, Florence was like a jewel set in a ring of softly molded hills. I looked at it a long time and came to the conclusion that it was unpaintable. There was too much beauty right there, on the surface. I thought of New York, huge, unwieldy, unmanageable, where I have been living

55

all my adult life and where my art was formed. There one has to scrape and dig to find beauty. It may well be to the good, I thought, from the artist's point of view.

While Mrs. Alexander was preparing dinner and talking with Rebecca, I made a drawing of Sidney with a framed reproduction of a fragment from Michelangelo in the background—the hand of God touching the hand of Adam, just the two hands. Sidney lives Michelangelo and his times. He told me of the great privilege he had been given, when through a secret passage he was permitted one day to ascend to the Sistine ceiling and examine the paintings at close range. "It was a great experience," he said. He made an exhaustive study of all of Michelangelo's work—in sculpture, painting, architecture. He has a great knowledge of the drawings, and considers Michelangelo as great a poet as he was a painter and sculptor. He doesn't think that Michelangelo was a homosexual. "Da Vinci yes, Michelangelo no." His long life was spent in a man's world, Sidney argued. He was always among men—his father and brothers, nephews, men servants. In the main, all his energy and sex drive simply went into his work. He lived a sexless life. He was aware that he was different, was troubled about it, but could not escape from himself. In one of the sonnets he prayed, "Make me want to want, O Lord, what I do not want." His identification was with the Old Testament rather than with the New. Except for the Madonnas and the Pietas, the bulk of his work was inspired by the Old Testament—the Sistine ceiling, the David, the Moses. He never carved a Christ on the Cross or a St. John the Baptist. I listened to Sidney with fascination.

At the table our conversation turned to their beloved Florence, which we are leaving tomorrow for Rome. I mentioned my regret that I would miss seeing Manzu in Rome and at my probably not finding Guttuso, who is rumored to be in the Soviet Union at this time. I also mentioned my regret in not having made drawings of Sartre and Aragon, whom I admired, when I was in Paris. A friend of theirs promised to send me introductions to them but neglected to do so.* I hoped to make a few portrait drawings in Rome. "I would like to do a drawing of, say, Moravia, whose *Two Women, The Two Adolescents* and the *Roman Tales* I read and liked a lot," I said. Whereupon Sidney said, "Moravia and I have the same literary agent. I'll give you her

* Actually these letters of introduction were written by Hannah Josephson and sent to my London hotel where I neglected to leave a forwarding address. Some months later these letters came back to New York to Mrs. Josephson.

56

telephone; I am sure she will be able to arrange a meeting for you with Moravia."

After dinner the four of us went to the Piazza Signoria and at an outdoor cafe table met the Gillettes, who have been living in Rome these past months. Henry Gillette, an ex-student of mine, was passing through Florence on the way to Milano to get additional material for the children's book he is doing on Leonardo Da Vinci, both the text and the illustrations. Henry knew Sidney Alexander's volume on Michelangelo and wondered what effect on him and his work the publication of *The Agony and the Ecstasy* had. Sidney said that he is almost finished with the second volume of his projected trilogy on Michelangelo. He praised Irving Stone, the author of *The Agony and the Ecstasy,* as a skillful writer, as a man who knows his craft.

July 27

At the Uffizi to look once more at the paintings before leaving for Rome in the afternoon. In the Dutch Room we met the elderly and active New York councilman, Stanley M. Isaacs and Mrs. Isaacs, eager, intelligent, keenly interested in the paintings, and later in the Rubens Room, the art collector Eric Cohn and his wife. A few days before my flight to Europe, Rebecca and I had been invited to the Cohns to dinner, and had the second opportunity (we had been there once before) to see their art collection. It is an interesting and personal one, mostly of works by German artists, Corinth, Grosz, Kollwitz; also some paintings by Floch, Menkes, Kars and others. His Grosz collection is particularly good.

Grosz is one of the artists of my time who never ceases to fascinate me . . . his draftsmanship, his powers of observation and trained memory. His drawings and prints of the so-called dada period are viciously expressive. Compared to them, Paul Klee's schizophrenic drawings seem like poetic doodles. The impact of George Grosz's work, it seems to me, lies in his power to identify himself with the characters he drew —all his characters, the villains as well as the victims. He himself is in turn the gluttonous, swine-like warmonger, the murderous Nazi, the tortured progressive, the striking worker, the degraded woman and the hungry child. He must have experienced, to a hallucinating degree, the sensations of sadism, masochism, the feelings of humiliation, anger, passion, but seldom pity. It is interesting to compare Kollwitz and Grosz. There are no heroes in Grosz's work, only villains and victims—he draws them with equal intensity. There is no element of compassion, or sympathy there; it is biting, cruel, viciously satirical. Kathe Kollwitz's work is a constant almost monotonously repetitious hymn to her hero—the masses, exploited, poverty-stricken, ravaged by death. She never, as far as I know, drew a military figure or a "capitalist."

George Grosz influenced many American artists: Shahn, Levine, Gropper, Baskin, and a host of the younger. Only Levine, as far as I know, publicly acknowledged his debt to Grosz.

Apropos George Grosz and Jack Levine, about a year and a half ago the argument arose at the American Institute of Arts and Letters as to whom to award the gold medal for graphic art—to George Grosz or to another candidate. One Institute member after another made a little speech to the effect that George Grosz was great in his youth but that his work deteriorated as he got older. The refrain was "George Grosz is not what he was." Finally, Jack Levine arose and looked with a kind of cold attention at the Institute members around him (most of them older than he) and said, "Who of us, with the exception of maybe Jonathan Swift, is what he was?"

July 31

This morning went to the Vatican to see the Michelangelo and the Raphael murals. Because of a cardinal's death the Vatican was closed for a few days. I consider the Sistine Chapel one of the three high points of my art pilgrimage—the other two being Rembrandt in Holland and Van Eyck in Belgium. As two years ago, we soon became part of the awe-stricken, astonished, bewildered, ecstatic crowd. That a man in his thirties could have painted the ceiling and many years later in his old age, the Last Judgment on the wall—natural organic continuation of the ceiling—single-handed! It is impossible to comprehend! Who could be compared with him?

I remembered how two years ago, the day we saw the Sistine Chapel for the first time, friends took us in the late afternoon to an art exhibition somewhere on an island in Trastevere. There they were again—

European and American non-objective paintings. To the charming girl at the desk we were introduced as an artist from New York and his wife. On the way out she looked at me and said something in Italian. "She is asking you 'What is your opinion of these paintings?'" my friend translated. After some hesitation I said, "Tell her that I saw the Sistine Chapel this morning." Her soft face clouded and she commented, "True, this does not speak to the heart."

Raphael's murals in the Vatican are pure joy to behold—his "School of Athens" in particular, with the magnificently drawn and posed figures.

August 1

I called Milton Hebald, the American sculptor who has been living and working in Rome for several years now, and soon found myself in his studio on the other side of the Tiber, facing it. "Paint here," Milton said. "Look at the view—the river, the trees, the beautiful architecture on the other bank. I even have an easel here for you." His sculptures in bronze, wood and plaster were scattered about—an ecstatic mother with a nude child clambering all over her, a sharp-kneed adolescent in skimpy skirt and amusing hat, nude men and women, singly or coupled. Talented, graceful, decorative work. He is one of the rare artists who enjoys commissions and has the knack of fulfilling them, with satisfaction to all concerned. In my mind was the first exhibition of his work I saw back in the nineteen-thirties—single figure pieces in neat white plaster, of people at work: a woman at a sewing machine, a shoemaker, etc. To this day I remember their simple and unpretentious quality.

In Paris Harry Jackson told me that he had met at a party someone who was introduced to him as Count-something-or-other, and who turned out to be the painter Balthus, whom Malraux appointed Director of the French Academy in Rome. Now, I know Balthus's painting well. "He is a sweet and intelligent guy," Harry said. "Call him up when you're in Rome, tell him you're a friend of Harry's."

I decided to call him right now. Milton helped me to get him on the phone. I soon heard Balthus's voice and told him that I was a New York artist, acquainted with his work and an admirer of it; that I was a friend of Harry Jackson and might I come and visit him. He asked me to come at 3 P.M. day after tomorrow for an hour. So much of his time, he said over the phone, was taken by his Academy duties. I asked if I might bring along my wife and my friend the sculptor, Hebald, who also knows his work. Balthus said, "Yes."

August 2

A few minutes before 3 P.M., Rebecca, Hebald and I were at the gates of the French Academy above the Spanish steps. We were ushered into a small elevator and taken to a spacious, columned portico. As in many Roman mansions and palaces, the important and beautiful part of the Academy was in the rear. We faced a cultivated park and below us were the Borghese Gardens. In niches along the portico walls of yellow ochre were antique marble figures. It was almost oppressively beautiful, timeless and still. I became moody. I looked at my wrist watch; it was almost twenty after. Finally, Mr. Balthus appeared, out of a side door, a thin, aristocratic-looking man. I had the feeling that he had had a nap and shaved himself before he made his appearance.

I introduced myself, Rebecca and Hebald. We conversed haltingly and politely. He told us that his Academy duties were heavy and kept him from painting as much as he would want to. He said that it takes him a long time to do a painting. My wife looked nervously at me and her eyes said, "Get your sketchbook out, time is passing. Come, tell him you want to make a sketch of him." I finally did, and he sat without moving, a glazed look in his eyes, unconsciously and imperceptibly raising his finely chiselled face higher and higher. "Your face makes me think of Chopin," I said. (Actually I wanted to say Mitzkewitch, but the name of the Polish poet escaped me that moment and I said Chopin.) "Have you ever painted a self-portrait, Mr. Balthus?" asked Hebald. "Yes," said Balthus. I ventured to tell that I knew he introduced his own likeness in his "Wuthering Heights" illustrations. "Yes, yes," he readily responded, "long ago, when I was young."

I took special pains to draw this handsome aristocratic, thin-blooded man and his finely featured face as accurately as I possibly could, not to err in proportion or to make an unnecessary line, for there was so little time left in which to do him, and to add further to my discomfiture, I'd forgotten to bring along my eraser. In the background I sketched in a classically robed marble figure in a niche. I showed my drawing to him and he smiled thinly. It won the approval of Milton Hebald and of course my wife.

August 3

This year again we visited the Fosse Ardeatina. The Hebalds took us to the cave, or series of caves, along the Appian Way where during the war the Nazis murdered 330 Italians in reprisal for 33 Germans blown up by partisans. They were Italian political prisoners, ordinary working men, merchants, etc.; 100 were of the Jewish faith. There was one boy of fourteen. The Nazis mowed them down with machine guns, blew up the cave with explosives, and left the bodies there in the wreckage. After the war, the Italian Government had the bodies removed from the rubble, identified most of them, placed each one in a marble coffin and the 330 coffins were set inside the cave which had been cleared and enlarged for this purpose, with a marble slab as a ceiling over the entire area. On each coffin there is a photograph with the name, age and occupation of the murdered man. The Christian coffins are marked with a cross, the Jewish ones with the Star of David. They are placed in aisles on raised platforms, to about table-height, and at the foot of each one there is a perpetual memorial light.

Outside the cave there is a simple landscaped clearing separated from the road by Mirco's sculptured, wrought-iron gate. A heroic monument of white stone depicting three men standing back to back with interlocked arms, supporting one another, looms high above the gate, stark white against the blue sky. High above the entrance to the cave are the two religious symbols—the Crucifix and the Star of David.

It is ironical that the guide books no longer recommend visits to this cemetery; the public touring buses do not include it in their itineraries, as they used to, because of a tacit agreement not to offend the present German government. Very few tourists know about Fosse Ardeatina, although multitudes of them visit the Catacombs a very short distance away.

We walked up and down the aisles and exchanged comments in hushed voices and looked at the photographed faces of these victims of the Nazis. Some coffins were marked "Unknown" because the bodies were so mangled that they could not be identified. There were a few other visitors in the cave, some relatives of the killed ones, who brought their children with them and laid flowers on coffins. A small group of women led by a monk came in.

We left the dimly-lit cave and stepped out into the sunlight and when we got back to the road we heard from a short distance away gutteral exclamations of "Ja wohl" and noisy laughter, and saw a gay and arrogant group of Germans led by a guide enter the ancient Catacombs. We had a strong desire to pull them into the Fosse Ardeatina.

August 4

This morning called up Gabriella Drudi, Moravia's literary agent, saying that I am an artist from New York, that I am traveling about Europe, keeping a kind of diary, both in words and pictures, that I have met and have made drawings of some artists and writers. I asked if it would be possible to meet Moravia and make a drawing of him. I added that Sidney Alexander suggested that I call her. Her answer surprised me: "Call him yourself. I'll give you his telephone number. He's probably home now." I called Moravia immediately. He spoke in an impatient tone of voice, and told me to call him Friday morning.

August 5

We were early for our afternoon appointment with Carlo Levi, whose house is somewhere off Piazza del Popolo. So we went into the Church of Santa Maria del Popolo to look at the Caravaggios. A genius again—a romantic and a realist—a Courbet and a Delacroix in one. The street to Carlo Levi's winds off the Piazza through a gate, to a woodsy park where his house stands in a grove of young willows. A hollow-cheeked, thin elderly housekeeper with beautifully set eyes let us into the disorderly anteroom. There were books on the shelves, on the chairs, on the floor, in Italian, in English, in French, some in Russian. On a huge

table was a vast confusion of books again, paintings, drawings, reproductions, dried flowers and leaves and twigs, and among all this a plaster
cast of a woman's head, her patient and meek face wrapped in a real
black shawl, some of the leaves and flowers strewn about it.

Levi came into the anteroom, escorting a young man out, and asked
us into the studio. It was a large room with more books and many more
drawings. There were stairs leading to a balcony where his living and
sleeping rooms are. One look at Carlo Levi fills one with friendliness
toward him. His is an expansive and exuberant personality. He told us
that the young man who just left came to enlist his interest in a new experimental theatre venture. "One must help them," he said, more to
himself than to us.

The many paintings were mostly of people: men, women and children. There was something generalized and symbolic about them, with
feverishly glowing eyes in hollow faces. The landscapes seemed to us of
southern Italy—barren and poor. The colors were somber gray, black,
ochre. There was a good deal of the writer in the paintings. The technique, however, was professional, spirited, painter-like. He showed
photos and slides of a huge composition he'd lately completed which was
being exhibited in Turin at this time. Turin is the section of Italy Levi
comes from, and is the locale of this painting, and the main figure, the
hero, was a poet and a dear friend of his youth. He is depicted a few
times in this mural-like composition, first teaching and lecturing to the
populace which is shown flocking to him on foot, on mules, in carts,
old and young, a modern variation on the "St. John the Baptist Preach-
ing" theme. Then it shows this poet leading the people in a strike or
in some struggle against oppression, and finally dying surrounded by
grief-stricken followers.

"This is my tribute to my friend," Levi said. The word "friend"
appeared often in his vocabulary. "Guttuso? Why, he is my dear and
intimate friend," he exclaimed. He has many friends in America. He
mentioned his friend Ben Shahn, with whom he spent some time a few
weeks ago. We told him that we saw his paintings in the Museo dell'Arte
Moderna and liked his youthful self-portrait and a head of an old man.
"The old man was my friend, the great Italian poet Saba," he said with
feeling. "He died a few years ago."

I wasn't able to do Levi justice in my drawings. I failed to capture
his aliveness. But then he posed badly. There were too many distrac-
tions. The telephone rang, he gave orders to his housekeeper: When
so-and-so comes for a contribution for some cause, make out the check.

63

He changed the position he was sitting in to stroke his big fluffy cat that passed by, and then a miserable little kitten that strayed in from the street; he told the housekeeper to give it food. He looked at the drawings of the artists in my sketchbook. They were his friends: "That's good of Zadkine," he said. "He, with many others, signed the statement protesting my imprisonment." He told us to go to Turin to see the exhibition there. He invited us to call and come again, and took down our address, with the idea of looking us up when he comes to New York.

August 6

This morning called Moravia again. I said, "I am the New York artist who wants to meet you and make a drawing of you. I called you a few days ago and you told me to call you this morning." "All right," Moravia said hurriedly, "come today at 7:30 P.M." Now, we had an invitation for this evening to the wedding reception of Hebald's daughter, and therefore I said, "Mr. Moravia, may I come at seven, because I have a later appointment this evening?" "All right, all right," was the hurried, impatient answer, "come at seven."

Promptly at 7 P.M. Rebecca and I rang the bell on the top floor of a modern apartment building, just off the Piazza del Popolo. A typical Italian housekeeper, middle-aged, with deep-set friendly eyes, let us in and asked us if we had an appointment with Mr. Moravia. We said yes, and she left us to inform him that we were there. Well, we waited ten, fifteen, twenty, twenty-five minutes. Two silent fluffy cats moved noiselessly to and fro and every time they passed us, arched their backs for us to scratch them. It was oppressively warm. We went out on the terrace. Rebecca examined the plants and flowers and plucked off wilted leaves. We went back into the room, and still there was no Moravia. It was half-past seven, and getting dark. "Rebecca, let's go," I said angrily, when the door opened and the housekeeper came in, saw us in the twilight of the room, still waiting. She clapped her hands in dismay and went out, saying dramatically in Italian what probably meant that she had told Moravia about the appointment, but that he gets so engrossed in his writing that he forgets everything.

In about two minutes the door opened abruptly and Moravia limped in. He is a tall, thin, lame man (we were told subsequently that he had

had infantile paralysis) with small eyes under bushy eyebrows, big flat nose, and thin mouth. His appearance was that of a retired baseball player. His behavior was as rough as his appearance. He said to me, completely ignoring Rebecca, in his hurried, informal manner: "You're the artist from New York. You'll have to draw me in my work room while I type." "May I come too, Mr. Moravia?" said Rebecca. "Well, the room is small," he answered ungraciously. "All right, all right, come."

The room was small, air-conditioned, with shelves of books by Tolstoi, Balzac, Stendhal and other famous authors. He sat at a huge table, cluttered with books, papers, manuscripts. He pointed to the sofa for me to sit down, from where I could draw him in profile only. Rebecca sat down next to me and began to read a newspaper she had with her. Moravia then commenced to pound his portable typewriter, I to draw, and to become witness to a strange metamorphosis.

Moravia's appearance changed. There seemed nothing crude about him any more. The light blue shirt clung softly to his shoulders and back. His profile, slightly lowered at his work, assumed an exterior and inner beauty. His head was well sculptured, with skull, forehead, nose, mouth, chin, ear, finely carved. His ear made me think of Tolstoi's ear, the way Maxim Gorky described it somewhere: "big, well-shaped, the kind writers have, the kind I remember Chekhov had." His profile expressed benignity, repose, contemplation; it had an inner glow, to use a hackneyed phrase. He worked with great concentration, and was also aware that I was drawing him, and held his pose. He typed with two fingers of one hand and with one finger of the other. Now and then he would stop typing for a minute, shade his eyes or rub his forehead with a well-shaped hand, and read what he had written. I realized that this man can work long periods of time, forgetful of everything about him. Rebecca read the first page of the newspaper over and over again. She didn't want to create noise by turning the newspaper pages. The muffled ticking of the typewriter was the only sound in the room.

Finally I closed my sketchbook, got up and said, "Thank you very much, Mr. Moravia, for letting me draw you. I feel we have intruded upon you." Moravia quickly got up, too. "I want to see the drawing," he said. I handed him the book, he quickly turned the pages. "Ah, Carlo Levi," he muttered to himself, under his breath. Finally he came upon the drawing of himself. He looked at it for a moment and smiled with approval. He said that we had not intruded upon him, but that he was pressed for time, and that he had to finish the piece he was doing. He escorted us to the door and warmly (it seemed to me) shook our hands.

"He liked your drawing," Rebecca exclaimed excitedly in the hallway. "He smiled—he really smiled when he saw the portrait you made of him. But, you want to know something, it occurs to me now that in all the portraits I saw in the newspapers, and on book jackets, of Moravia, he is always in profile."

We went from there to the beautiful apartment of Milton and Cecile Hebald, for the wedding reception of their daughter Margo. It took place on the terrace, dimly lit by candles set in lamp chimneys. Below were canyon-like narrow streets, and from the yellow, flat facades of the old buildings gaped blindly open, curtainless windows. Met John Manship there, a painter, son of Paul Manship.

August 7

I knew that Eugene Berman lives in Rome. Rebecca and I met him two years ago at a party George Biddle gave in his studio at the American Academy. He told me then that Rome is the city he loves; if I remember correctly, he naturally and simply said, "Rome is my city," and he chose to live there. A few months later I saw him in New York at Knoedler's Gallery where there was an exhibition of his paintings. Their theme was Rome. I called him to tell him we were here in Rome, and might we visit him? He very readily invited us to come Sunday and have lunch with him.

We were overwhelmed by Berman's friendliness. He occupies two apartments, one above the other, in the Palazzo Doria. Both places are veritable museums filled with antique, Gothic, African sculpture, icons, engravings, his own paintings and drawings, and paintings and drawings by his contemporaries and friends. We sat in the shade on a beautiful terrace and he served us drinks. He is a fine conversationalist. He reminisced some about his past and his cultural background in Czarist Russia, especially about his life and art in Paris, where he emigrated during the First World War. I made a drawing of him sitting at a round table in one of the art-filled rooms.

He then took us down to his favorite restaurant nearby and with the suave assurance of a worldly gourmet ordered our food. His every whim was eagerly catered to by a friendly and respectful waiter who seemed to admire his tastes.

We continued to converse and Berman talked interestingly and feelingly about his friends, Paul Chelichev and Christian Bérard, who, with him, his brother Leonid and a few others, had founded the Neo-Romantic or Neo-Humanist movement in Paris. The group held exhibitions which attracted a great deal of attention. Both Chelichev and Bérard died not too many years ago. I think Berman said that of the whole group only he and Leonid are alive today. He talked about plans to organize and hold a historical exhibition of paintings by the Neo-Humanists in New York. I hope that this exhibition will take place. It would interest many to see the early works by these talented artists. I know some of these paintings—melancholy, moody, poetic, perverse. I would call Picasso's early blue paintings Neo-Humanistic. The work of Balthus, too. More about Chelichev and Bérard. Berman described how both, each in his own way, mistreated their talents. Bérard took his too lightly, and dissipated it by doing all sorts of trivial work. Chelichev, on the contrary, overestimated his talent and attempted the grandiose and unattainable, finally losing himself in metaphysics.

It was late afternoon when we said good-by to Eugene Berman. There was something essentially lonely about this cultured, gifted, whimsical and capricious man, in spite of his many international friendships and connections.

August 8

With my sister Fannie and her husband Dr. Isaac Mendelsohn, and the young artist Marcial Rodriguez and his wife Electa, we wandered about old Rome—the Coliseum, the Forum, etc. The Arch of Titus impressed me by its authenticity.

Spent a couple of hours again at Galeria Nazionale d'Arte Moderna in one of the several beautiful buildings in the Borghese Gardens. This museum is analogous to the Whitney Museum of American Art in New York City. It houses a very comprehensive collection of nineteenth and twentieth century Italian paintings and sculpture. All the tendencies are shown, all shades of representationalism and non-representationalism. There wasn't the feeling of favoritism of one tendency over the other that one is aware of in the American museums. There seems to be an effort on the part of the directors to be fair to all decent artists of Italy today, no matter what their artistic persuasion is. Nor were the nineteenth century narrative paintings discarded and put away in cellars, as often happens in American museums, where, at the whim of directors, works of art out of immediate fashion are often even sold at auction.

There were some very interesting internationally-known paintings by the futurists and the so-called metaphysical painters; a group of paintings by Casorati, an artist whose work has always attracted me, and paintings by many others. Of the artists more or less of my generation, I was again impressed by the vigor of Guttuso. There was a youthful, already masterful work of his—people fleeing the erupting Etna, a violent, dramatic work. Another painting was of a group of female nudes drawn and painted with great intensity.

There were three paintings by Carlo Levi I liked, especially his youthful self-portrait, and a head of an old man. An interesting group of expressionistic paintings by Scipione, an artist who died very young. Also paintings by Corrado Cagli, Mafai, Zigana and others. All artists were represented by several paintings, some by as many as five or more.

It goes without saying that abstraction and non-objectivism are also here in force. There were some pleasant decorations among them, tasteful in color and shapes. But most of the paintings in this large, high-ceilinged room were wild; their one objective seemed to be to attract attention. In spite, or because of this, there was a sense of anonymity about them. All the paintings seemed the same. Their authors seem to have lost their individual identities and their identities as artists as well. They are not painting any more, they are perpetrating acts of something or other—some of them say so themselves.

I was impressed by the early sculpture of Marino Marini, the portraits and the bronze nude, an excellent collection of work by Manzu—of his cardinals, dancers, the Crucifixion reliefs, and finally a whole room of Madordo Rossi's impressionistic, delicate, fugitive sculpture.

August 10

Corrado Cagli's studio is set in an old wall across the way from the ancient ruins on Circo Massimo. We got there late because we were misdirected a few times, and it took a lot of circling about till we finally got there and found Cagli and a younger man standing like two sentinels at the doorway waiting for us. Corrado Cagli introduced the young man as a pupil of his. The walls of the small anteroom were hung with his collection of drawings by his contemporaries and by artists of earlier times. I recognized Eugene Berman's, Guttuso's and Mirco's drawings among others. Also a drawing by the nineteenth-century artist Mancini.

He told us that he has a big collection of paintings by young artists who are or were his students. He is one painter who takes his teaching very seriously. In the course of the evening I realized that there was a master and disciple relationship between him and the serious-looking young man.

Unassuming, unspectacular, one cannot mistake Cagli for anything but the artist he is. There is something warm and self-contained about his bearing. He spoke briefly to his student, who brought out from the racks a group of canvases and, at his master's orders, placed them on the easel, one by one. The first was a portrait done quite representationally and muted in color. Then some gouaches, very beautiful ones, preliminary studies for a mosaic for a fountain, depicting fishermen and fishing.

Most of his present work, however, was semi- or completely abstract. Some of these paintings in color, light and form were evocative of Roman walls and ruins. We told him this, and he was pleased. All over the studio, on tables, on shelves attached to walls, were some kind of sculptures, consisting of pieces of cardboard or thin plastic, tacked or taped together, in shapes of abstracted heads and figures—eventually to be cast in bronze.

Cagli speaks English well, for he lived in the States and during the

Second World War served in the American Army and was decorated for valor. Now he chooses to be an Italian citizen again. We talked about art in America and Italy. One remark I thought significant, that some Italian artists, the moment they begin to sell in America, become snobs. He named some of them. But he spoke warmly about Guttuso, Eugene Berman, Carlo Levi, and others. I was impressed especially by what he said about Carlo Levi, that at times he tends to be indolent and lax, but that in times of stress and need he is a great and trusted friend. He asked about American artists he knew when in the U.S., about Ed Melcarth and others.

Later, Cagli took us in a taxi to the huge studio where workers help him with his mosaic. It was quite unfinished as yet, but already very beautiful in design and color of ochres, browns, Venetian reds, dull blacks and blues. Only one of the workers was in the shop, and we liked the friendliness and the respect he displayed toward Cagli. The walls of the shop were entirely covered by Cagli's collection of work by young artists, some of them his students and ex-students. He buys their paintings. He invited us to visit him again, and I said that we would come and that I would bring my sketchbook along to make a drawing of him.

August 11

This morning visited Orvieto. At the station, went up in the funicular to the old city, perched high up on the mountain. It is a completely charming town, not as forbidding as Siena had appeared to me. The cathedral of white and black striped marble was truly beautiful and impressive, with its facade decorated with naive, amusing and gruesome carvings in relief, illustrating events described in the Old and New Testaments, such as the Creation, Adam and Eve in Paradise, their expulsion, the Passion of Christ, the Last Judgment, etc. In a side chapel of the pleasantly unobstructed and spacious church are, of course, the Signorelli frescoes. They are unusually well preserved. The color is clear and bright.

Besides the beauty that European cities have—the historical flavor about them and their museums—they possess the wonderful institution of the outdoor cafe. In the late afternoons we usually found ourselves in one of these cafes overlooking the Seine in Paris, or on the Boulevard Montparnasse, in the Piazza Signoria in Florence, or here in Rome in the Piazza del Popolo or the friendly Piazza Navona, which especially endeared itself to us. We walked to it this afternoon from our hotel situated in the Via Veneto section of the city. We took our time and wandered leisurely in and out of the non-touristy side streets and alleys. Dark, windowless cavelike shops gaped like holes in the plain facades of ancient ochre buildings. Little groups of local men and women sat out-of-doors at rectangular wooden tables, not the round plastic cafe ones, eating, drinking, carrying on lively conversation. Intimate couples stood in doorways; messenger boys and girls, some of them mere children, dressed in black smocks (how I would love to draw them!) went about their errands. "Gee, it is much more interesting here than around the Via Veneto," Rebecca would say from time to time.

In the middle of the Piazza, on benches, on the long rectangular raised pavement, sat old men and women reading their papers, boys and girls having fun with one another, and a young mother who bared her breast to feed her baby. Around the Bernini fountains, children jumped rope and played other games known to children all over the world. There are no cars to disturb these people—traffic is restricted to a narrow road around this raised pavement. On the other side of this road are the warm-colored houses, the balconies decorated with flower pots, mostly geraniums, the restaurants and the cafes, and all this bathed in soft Italian late afternoon light. We sat down at a table at one of the cafes, sipped our drinks, rested from our walk, and I sketched.

Rebecca and I were at the Colosseum. It is impossible to describe the blue Italian skies, especially in the late afternoon, and the effect of the luminous light upon the Colosseum walls. I made a drawing of a section of the wall with a side view of Rebecca sitting on the ruins of a low wall in the foreground. When I was almost through with the drawing, a boy of about eight sat down near Rebecca. In sign language I asked him to sit quietly a few minutes, which he did. When I showed him the finished drawing, the little boy smiled, shook my hand, and said, "Bravo."

August 14

A few hours after we left the deliciously hot and sunny Rome by plane, we found ourselves in rainy and chilly Amsterdam.

August 15

I have seen many paintings these months, yet here I was in the Rembrandt Room, gaping as though I had never seen a painting before, at the images of the man and the woman dressed in scarlet and gold, the intimacy between them conveyed by the moving gesture of their wonderful hands. How modern are the brush strokes, how like crusted lava the impasto, how smoldering the color! "The Jewish Bride" has been cleaned since we saw it two years ago, delicately cleaned, not violently scrubbed as they often do to paintings in America and England. We walked over to the portrait Rembrandt painted of himself in the role of St. Paul. "How old he looks! He lost his teeth!" Rebecca exclaimed softly in compassion, as if Rembrandt were a living and old friend, whom one hadn't seen for a long time, and now came upon him and found him sadly aged.

"The Syndics" is one of the two greatest portrait groups ever painted; the other is Velásquez's "Las Meninas" in the Prado.

"The Syndics" . . . words fail me. I am only a painter . . . I find it impossible even to myself to sensibly rationalize my emotion in front of this masterpiece. These men, these Dutch contemporaries of Rembrandt, who lived and probably died in Amsterdam, are timeless and universal.

The paintings are excellently displayed in the Rijksmuseum. Other great paintings there, besides the Rembrandts, are Vermeers, and the many Jan Steens. Frans Hals emerges here as an inimitable and original master. Sanredaam's church interiors in white, yellow ochre and brown; three interesting compositions by the fascinating Flemish master Joos Van Gent.

August 17

The Stedelijk Museum is enormous. Many activities go on at once. A tremendous Van Gogh exhibition, a show of recent Dutch paintings entitled "Holland 1961," a display of illustrated books for children, a photography exhibition, and more.

The one that interested me most was a theme exhibition called "Polaritet"—Polarity. The aim was to show that there are two strong pulls in Western art: the "Dionysian"—the Romantic—and the "Apollonian"—the classical. The exhibition begins with Ingres and Delacroix, continues with the French Impressionists, German Expressionists, then Munch, Ensor, Kokoschka, on to Paul Klee, Kandinsky, the other two Russians Malevich and Lissitzky, etc., and finally the non-objective painters of today. Not one representational painting after Mondrian. As if representational art had suddenly ceased to exist, at least as far as the arranger of this exhibition is concerned. All the paintings are neatly pigeonholed into the Romantic and the Classical compartments. The Romantic paintings are hung in partitioned sections on one side of the room and the Classical on the other side. In the aisle between the Classical and the Romantic paintings are two canvases by the unclassifiable Picasso, who is used here as the proverbial exception to prove the rule, and thus add to the validity of the show. His cruelly distorted painting of a nude is, of course, Romantic, and the other one of a Hellenistic head of a woman Classical. In the pandemonium of non-objectivism are a couple of American paintings—a Romantic one and a Classical one.

There were some interesting paintings by Cézanne, Seurat, Kokoschka and others, and a most beautiful study by Delacroix for "Crusaders Entering Contantinople," which is in the Louvre. But all in all this thematically planned exhibition, constructed as it was to present some theory, seemed to me very much like someone's Ph.D. thesis to

73

prove his claim to erudition. This type of exhibition is frequent and fashionable today. Every young museum director who wants to make his debut, and every assistant museum director who has to prove his worth arranges one.

Whatever my opinion of the "Polaritet" show was, I could not help but ask myself: "Where do I belong? How do I fit in, in today's art world?" I have been aware these many years as a practicing artist of the changes in our world, our life, in art, in aesthetics. Surely I have changed, too, and my art is different today from what it was, say, in the late nineteen twenties. My representational paintings I am certain reflect to some extent our civilization, our time, our moment. Yet my work is not to be found these days in "Polaritet" sort of exhibitions, nor in the sumptuous and empty international displays in the United States, Brazil, Italy for that matter. I fondly hope that this is so, not because I have been unable to keep "abreast of the times" as an artist, but because I have resolved years ago to paint the way it pleases me— representationally, for better or for worse. If non-representationalism, I then said to myself, is the only art of our time, I would rather not belong, artistically, to our time. Did not Ingres once exclaim in anger, "They (his detractors) say that I am not of the century. If I do not like my century, must I belong to it?"

August 19

We were charmed by the old cobbled streets lined with white and brown gabled houses of Amsterdam, by the many tree-lined canals which add sparkle and light to the city, by the parklike squares. We sat for long periods at a time in outdoor cafes and watched with fascination the stern and confident profiles of the swarms of cyclists of all ages, male and female. The city itself seems to have a face, an honest and open one. The most impressive square, "The Dam," is dominated by a monument to the resistance fighters during the Nazi occupation. At the base of this monument and around it gather the local teen-agers in their faded tight jeans and sloppy sweaters.

On a large market square in the working-class section called the "Waterloo Plein" is another monument. This one is in memory of the Jewish victims of Nazism. And of course we visited the Rembrandt house, old churches, the synagogue . . . and the famous red-light district.

August 22

It rained practically every day of our two-weeks' stay in Holland. But our activities were not curtailed a bit. In the Hague we saw more Rembrandts of all periods of his life. His earliest, or one of his earliest self-portraits and his last self-portrait are there, and Vermeer's "Young Girl" and "View of Delft." We went to Haarlem, of course, to see the Frans Hals group portraits. We were impressed particularly by the two paintings he did in his old age, when he was eighty-two years old, to be exact, one of a group of old men, and one of old women. They lack, needless to say, the technical bravado of his earlier works. Spiritually, however, they are on a higher level. There is a meaningful and expressive poverty of color about these two disturbing works. The faces and the many hands seem strangely scattered, the hands especially seem to flutter restlessly all over the two canvases.

In Rotterdam another fine museum with more Rembrandts, an early and rare Van Eyck, and my favorite Hieronymus Bosch of the "Prodigal Son."

Rotterdam is a new city. It is still in the process of being rebuilt since its devastation by the Nazis. On the square overlooking the harbor is Ossip Zadkine's monument to the Resistance. It looms dramatically against the swiftly moving clouds of the sky. This heroic but completely perforated and fragmented figure seemed to us the very symbol of accusation and anger. It is in bronze, and will last long.

We went by train from Amsterdam to Arnheim, and then by bus to the Kröller-Müller Museum where we saw another mammoth collection of paintings by Vincent Van Gogh, work by French Impressionists, and by Munch, Ensor, Kokoschka, and the inevitable Picassos, Braques, Miros, Mondrians, etc. There is a wonderful adjoining sculpture park studded with bronzes by Rodin, Maillol, Bourdelle, Henry Moore, Zadkine, Lipshitz, Manzu, Marino Marini, Giacometti, and many others. There are many such parks in Holland and Belgium and probably other countries but not once did I see a sculpture by an American.

75

We came to the Anne Frank house, walking to it from our hotel. As usual, although we had a map, we had to ask our way several times. Everyone knew where the house was, and seemed to take a personal interest in our desire to visit it. One shoemaker left his bench and went out with us into the street to show us more clearly where to go.

We climbed up the very steep and narrow stairway to the two upper floors of this old warehouse, grasping the steps with our hands, and found ourselves in an entirely empty room. In fact, all the rooms were terribly bare and empty. There were an old iron cookstove, a sink, the water closet in the hall. Everything else had been looted by the Nazis. The only sign of Anne Frank's presence in this melancholy place were her pinups on the wall in the room where she slept. They were typical of any thirteen- or fourteen-year-old girl's pinups—pictures of handsome young men, actors, ballerinas, of the Queen, of the Royal Family. Yellow and brittle with age, they were covered by glass to preserve them.

August 28

(the last lap of our
European journey)

We are in Antwerp. The Excelsior Hotel, opposite the railroad station, the Zoo, and not far from the waterfront, will be our headquarters for the few days we will spend in Belgium.

August 29

At the Antwerp Museum—the Van der Weydens, Van der Goes, the Van Eycks, and the Memlings are the gems here. The wonderful unfinished panel of St. Barbara by Van Eyck, a miraculous drawing, really, just the upper part tentatively touched by color. The "Seven Sacraments" by Rogier Van der Weyden, a vertical composition of a fantastically rendered interior of a Gothic cathedral, with the typically wonderfully-drawn (I am tempted to say Flemish-ly drawn) lamenting female figures in the foreground. And many of those small self-contained composed portraits by Van der Weyden, Van der Goes, Memling, Bouts and other masters. I didn't care particularly for the huge and sumptuous Rubenses here.

We went into the great Cathedral for which Rubens painted his famous "Descent from the Cross," the "Crucifixion" and the "Ascension." The "Descent" was not here. There was a plaque saying that it had been removed temporarily for restoration. The interior of this Cathedral seemed exactly like the one in Van der Weyden's painting, "The Seven Sacraments"—stark, white, extremely Gothic.

Near the Cathedral Square is the busy waterfront and a very interesting park with long rows of benches facing each other under strange, gnarled stumpy trees. All the benches were occupied, mostly by elderly middle-aged men and women, by couples with children, but not too many younger people. All of them seemed to be rather poor and drab. We found a place to sit down and I made my last European drawing.

August 30

Came to Ghent by bus in the morning and immediately went to St. Bavon's Cathedral to see the Van Eyck altarpiece. Going on that morning, there was a funeral of an important citizen, evidently, for the Cathedral was filled with the mourners. The matronly woman who was in charge of the Van Eyck Chapel was plainly involved with the funeral, to the extent that she neglected her duties. She would leave her post every so often to listen to the eulogies, and would return with tear-filled eyes and an absent-minded expression on her face.

To me this altarpiece of the Van Eyck brothers is one of the culminating works of Western art of all time. It is mysterious, supernatural, superhuman. All the aspects of the real and the spiritual are mastered here. The figures of Adam and Eve sent a shiver down my spine—so authentically and fatally human are they. Unfortunately, the altarpiece is overilluminated by floodlights.

As we were going out, we met Benjamin Sonnenberg, the art collector, about to enter the chapel. He greeted us as if he had seen us yesterday—

77

we met him last about five years ago in Truro. "Is my son there?" he asked, matter-of-factly. We didn't know he had a son. "A Christlike young man with a beard?" "Oh, yes, I did see a young man with a beard, looking at Van Eyck with great intensity," Rebecca said.

Later on Mr. Sonnenberg joined us at the cafe on the square.

"What does your son do?" I asked.

"Well," he answered, "my son is what my mother would call in Yiddish a '*leidig-geher*,'—a do-nothing. He is an aesthete. He has a feeling for cathedrals, museums and altarpieces such as this. He writes." Presently the young man joined us, thoughtful, obviously moved by the Van Eyck. He showed us a richly illustrated book, "L'Agneau Mystique," by Leo Van Puyvelde. When I expressed my admiration for it, he unexpectedly inscribed it:

> "For Raphael Soyer
> respectfully,
> Ben Sonnenberg, Jr."

and gave it to me.

And they went off to somewhere in the South of France, in quest of a famous cathedral.

September 1

Spent the whole day in Bruges. Walked from the pretentious and modernistic station along a modern road, both strangely out of character with the medieval town we soon entered, of cobbled streets, its low brick and plaster houses, its picturesque but dirty and smelly canals, and its cathedrals disproportionately huge.

At St. John's Hospital were the Memlings. What a portraitist Hans Memling was! The portrait of Martin Nieuwenhove, in a wonderful interior, with hands folded in prayer, and of two men and two women donors also with hands folded in prayer on the reverse side of the triptych "The Mystic Marriage of St. Catherine" are full of character, austere in color and composition.

In the Communal Museum again many detail-filled triptychs and altarpieces by Memling, Van der Goes, Van der Weyden, Gerard David, Dirk Bouts. One can study them endlessly. But the pièce de résistance in the Museum is Jan Van Eyck's monumental and architectural "The

Virgin and the Canon Van der Paele." The portrait of the Canon is one of the most searching and analytical ever painted. The infinitely detailed delineation of the features of the old man's face, every wrinkle of it, and of the pudgy hands that hold the prayer book and spectacles, of the texture of the eyes, of the white garment, are truly miraculous, as is the powerful drawing of the outline of the head. The psychological insight is extraordinary. How penetratingly Van Eyck expressed the anxiety of this man, his sense and fear of mortality!

September 3

We're in the jet homeward bound. I wonder how I will react this time to New York, after being in beautiful Europe almost four months. In 1959 when I came back, New York seemed impossible—park-less, café-less, harsh, impersonal. Men and women walked hard pavements silently, abstractedly. The Second and the Third Avenue bums depressed me. My work displeased me. I was melancholy for weeks and painted pictures of aimless, introverted pedestrians with masklike faces. It took time to get into stride.

I feel that I know Europe better this time, the famous European cities, at least, London, Paris, Rome, Amsterdam, etc. Of course I know them only as a tourist does, a tourist whose interests are limited to art, at that. My knowledge therefore is superficial. I had no time or inclination to penetrate beyond the facade of beauty and quaintness presented to the tourist, yet occasionally I did get an intimation of what was behind this facade. After visiting some families of European friends, I suddenly realized that the reason for so much public love-making in Paris or London, for instance, is the drabness and meanness of the homes of these young people. Their lack of privacy makes it necessary for them to seek each other out in streets, in parks, under bridges. What the tourist sees as a romantic aspect of European life is really a makeshift caused by necessity.

But as far as art is concerned I have had my fill. I have seen all I set out to see. I feel proud and content like a gourmet who ate well. This whole trip was really a pilgrimage to museums. I saw the bulk of the work of Rembrandt, who painted the human image in the center of the canvas as if it were the center of the universe; the altarpiece of Van

Eyck—that miraculous fusion of the infinitesimal with the infinite; the cycle of life and death in Michelangelo's Sistine Chapel; the timeless frescoes of Giotto, Masaccio and Piero della Francesca and the deeply disturbing altarpieces of Grünewald and Hugo Van der Goes. I am inspired. This is the heritage of the human spirit, the constructive, creative force of man which we must continue and extend if art is to survive. From all that I have seen I am more than ever convinced that art must communicate, it must represent, it must describe and express people, their lives and times.

Plates

83   *Detail from Rubens*

Detail from Rubens　　　　　　　　　　　　　　　　　　84

85

J. B. Bratby in London

Peter de Francis in London

J. B. Bratby in London

Henry Moore, Memory Drawing   88

Elgin Marbles

Susanna Bott in London   90

RAPHAEL SOYER · Paris 1961

Ossip Zadkine

John and Helen Dobbs, Paris   *92*

Park in Paris

Mrs. Kars in Paris   94

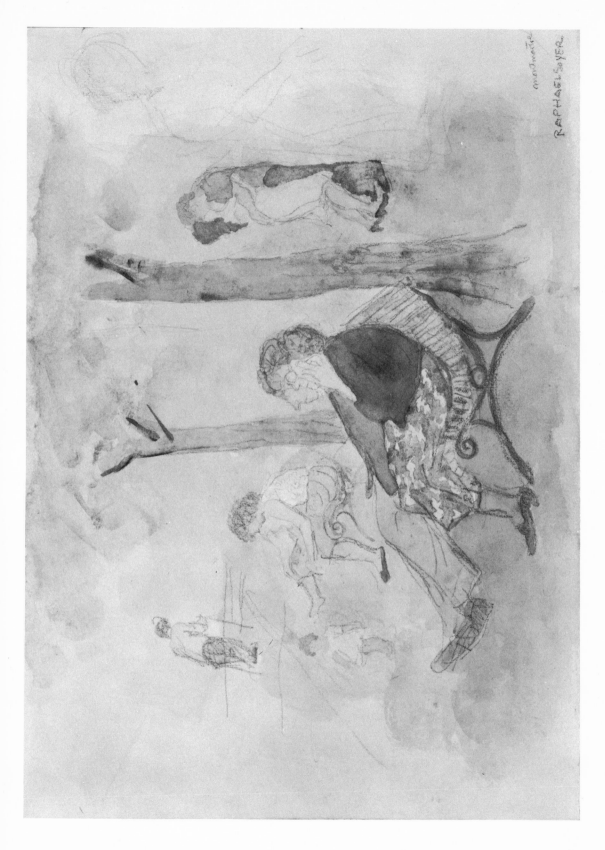

Park in Paris

From Raphael 96

Antonella da Messina

In a Hotel in Milan

99   *Pino Ponti, Milan*

Cadorin

Street in Venice

Florence

RAPHAËL SOYER ANTICOLI ITALY

A Hilltown in Italy

Pieta by Michelangelo in Duomo, Florence

Pieta in Duomo, Florence

David by Michelangelo

Grazzini and Son

Suttman and wife, Florence

Detail from Rubens in Florence

Milton Hebald

Red Grooms and Mimi Gross

Balthus

Piazza Navona, Rome

Piazza del Popolo, Rome

Piazza del Popolo, Rome

Carlo Levi

Moravia in Rome

Corrado Cagli

Eugene Berman

Piazza del Popolo, Rome

122

Wine Drinkers in Marino, Italy

Sidney Alexander

125   *Under the Resistance Monument, Amsterdam*

Rodin in a Rotterdam Museum

Park in Antwerp